Legal Provisions on Fighting Extremism

China • Pakistan • Russia • Tajikistan

The Law Library of Congress, Global Legal Research Center
(202) 707-6462 (phone) • (866) 550-0442 (fax) • law@loc.gov • http://www.law.gov

Contents

China 1

Pakistan 10

Russia 26

Tajikistan 45

Comparative Survey Chart...56

People's Republic of China

Laney Zhang
*Senior Foreign Law Specialist**

SUMMARY   China has not passed a comprehensive counterterrorism law. Counterterrorism provisions are mainly found in the Criminal Law and State Security Law. However, these laws do not provide a clear definition of "terrorism" or address extremism. In 2011, the country's top legislative body for the first time clearly defined the term "terrorist activities."

Domestically, extremism is more a politicized notion appearing in government instruments than a precisely defined legal term. In these instruments, extremism is linked with terrorism and separatism, which are rhetorically expressed as the "Three Forces" of "ethnic separatist forces, violent terrorist forces, and religious extremist forces." Extremism is addressed in very limited domestic legislation.

China has entered into the Shanghai Convention on Combating Terrorism, Separatism and Extremism, which provides a definition of "extremism" and requires that acts of extremism be criminally prosecuted in conformity with the national laws of the parties.

I. Background and Constitution

China does not have an anti-extremism law comparable to that of Russia and Tajikistan. A definition of "extremism" has not been found in domestic legislation, although the concept, as well as those of terrorism and separatism, are specifically defined by multilateral and bilateral treaties that China has entered into. Domestically, extremism is more a politicized notion appearing in government instruments than a precisely defined legal term.

Although counterterrorism provisions can be found in the Criminal Law and in a handful of other national laws such as the State Security Law, the country has not passed a comprehensive counterterrorism law; nor has "terrorism" been clearly defined by these laws. The government asserts it is premature to pass a single counterterrorism law. Instead, the Standing Committee of the National People's Congress (NPC), China's top legislative body, issued a decision in October 2011 specifically providing definitions of "terrorist organization," "terrorism," and "terrorist."[1]

The Chinese Constitution does not directly address extremism or terrorism. It contains, however, the following articles regarding "disruption of the social system," ethnic groups, and using religion to disrupt public order:

---

* This report was last updated in April 2014.

[1] *Zhongguo Zhubu Wanshan Fankong Fazhi Jianshe* [*China Gradually Establishing Counterterrorism Legal System*] (Nov. 29, 2011), NATIONAL PEOPLE'S CONGRESS, http://www.npc.gov.cn/npc/zgrdzz/2011-11/29/content_1680782.htm, *archived at* http://perma.cc/CH6W-CFEK.

Article 1. The socialist system is the basic system of the People's Republic of China. Disruption of the socialist system by any organization or individual is prohibited.

Article 4. Discrimination against and oppression of any ethnic groups are prohibited; any act which undermines the unity of the ethnic groups or instigates division is prohibited.

Article 36. No one may make use of religion to engage in activities that disrupt public order, impair the health of citizens or interfere with the educational system of the State.[2]

II. Counterterrorism Legislation

A. Criminal Law

As a response to the September 11, 2001, terrorist attacks on the US, China issued amendment III to its Criminal Law on December 29, 2001.[3] According to the NPC, the purposes of the amendment are "to punish the crimes of terrorism, to safeguard the security of the State and of people's lives and property, and maintain public order."[4]

Amendment III of the Criminal Law focused on articles addressing terrorist crimes and other crimes believed to endanger public security. The relevant punishments were increased and new provisions added. Most of the articles modified by Amendment III are under a chapter titled "Crimes of Endangering Public Security"—in particular article 120 addressing the crimes of organizing, leading, and participating in terrorist organizations. These articles have become the primary counterterrorism provisions in Chinese law.

The newly revised article 120 provides as follows:

> Whoever forms or leads a terrorist organization shall be sentenced to fixed-term imprisonment of not less than 10 years or life imprisonment; persons who actively participate in a terrorist organization shall be sentenced to fixed-term imprisonment of not less than 3 years but not more than 10 years; other participants shall be sentenced to fixed-term imprisonment of not more than 3 years, criminal detention, public surveillance or deprivation of political rights.[5]

Pursuant to Amendment III, a new sub-article 120a on funding terrorist organizations and individuals has been added to article 120 and provides:

> Whoever provides funds to any terrorist organization or individual who engages in terrorism shall be sentenced to fixed-term imprisonment of not more than five years,

---

[2] XIANFA arts. 1, 4, and 36 (1982, last amended Mar. 14, 2004), available in English translation *in* 2004 LAWS OF PEOPLE'S REPUBLIC OF CHINA 59, 70 (Legislative Affairs Commission of the Standing Committee of the National People's Congress (NPC); Beijing, 2005) [hereinafter LAWS OF CHINA].

[3] Amendment III to the Criminal Law of the People's Republic of China (Order of the President No. 64, Dec. 29, 2001) (Amendment III), 2001 LAWS OF CHINA 361–65.

[4] *Zhonghua Renmin Gongheguo Xingfa Xiuzheng An San Shiyi* [*Interpretation of Amendment III to the Criminal Law*] (Oct. 20, 2004), NATIONAL PEOPLE'S CONGRESS, http://www.npc.gov.cn/npc/flsyywd/xingfa/2004-10/20/content_337787.htm, *archived at* http://perma.cc/F93X-LH5K.

[5] Amendment III, 2001 LAWS OF CHINA 361–65.

criminal detention, public surveillance or deprivation of political rights, and shall also be fined; if the circumstances are serious, he shall be sentenced to fixed-term imprisonment of not less than five years, and he shall also be fined or his property shall be confiscated. Where a unit commits the crime mentioned in the preceding paragraph, it shall be fined, and the persons who are directly in charge and the other persons who are directly responsible for the offence shall be punished in accordance with the provisions of the preceding paragraph.[6]

The Criminal Law (including Amendment III), however, does not provide clear definitions of "terrorist organization" or "terrorism," nor does it specifically address extremism.

B. State Security Law

The State Security Law, another source of China's counterterrorism law, lists acts that are deemed to endanger state security in article 4, stating as follows:

> "Act endangering state security" as referred to in this Law means any of the following acts endangering the state security of the People's Republic of China committed by institutions, organizations or individuals outside the territory of the People's Republic of China, or, by other persons under the instigation or financial support of the aforementioned institutions, organizations or individuals, or, by organizations or individuals within the territory in collusion with institutions, organizations or individuals outside the territory:
> (1) plotting to subvert the government, dismember the State or overthrow the socialist system;
> (2) joining an espionage organization or accepting a mission assigned by an espionage organization or by its agent;
> (3) stealing, secretly gathering, buying, or unlawfully providing state secrets;
> (4) instigating, luring or bribing a State functionary to turn traitor; or
> (5) committing any other act of sabotage endangering state security.[7]

Terrorism is not expressly listed in the Law as one of these acts; however, the Implementation Rules of the State Security Law interpret the article 4 as encompassing terrorist activities. According to the Implementation Rules, "organizing, plotting or committing terrorist acts endangering the State security" falls into "any other act of sabotage endangering state security," referred to in article 4(5) of the State Security Law.[8] Like the Criminal Law, the State Security Law and its implementation rules do not provide a clear definition of "terrorist acts."

C. NPC Standing Committee Counterterrorism Decision

According to a statement posted on the NPC official website regarding the development of China's counterterrorism law system, there was previously no clear and precise definition of

---

[6] *Id.*

[7] Guojia Anquan Fa [State Security Law] (adopted by the NPC Standing Committee on Feb. 22, 1993, effective on the same day), art. 10, 1993 LAWS OF CHINA 43, 47.

[8] Guojia Anquan Fa Shishi Xize [Implementation Rules of State Security Law] (State Council Order [1994] No. 157, June 4, 1994), FALÜ FAGUI QUANSHU [LAWS AND REGULATIONS OF CHINA] 3–179.

"terrorist organizations," "terrorist activities," or "terrorists" provided in domestic law, and the lack of clear definitions hampered China's cooperation with international counterterrorism efforts.[9] The NPC filled this gap in 2011.

On October 29, 2011, the NPC Standing Committee passed the *Decision on Issues Related to Strengthening Counterterrorism Work*, which clarifies the definitions of "terrorist activities," "terrorist organizations," and "terrorist."[10] In the Decision, "terrorist activities" are defined as

> [a]ctivities that severely endanger society that have the goal of creating terror in society, endangering public security, or threatening state organs and international organizations and which, by the use of violence, sabotage, intimidation, and other methods, cause or are intended to cause human casualties, great loss to property, damage to public infrastructure, and chaos in the social order, as well as activities that incite, finance, or assist the implementation of the above activities through any other means.[11]

"Terrorist organizations" are defined as criminal organizations established for the purpose of carrying out terrorist activities. "Terrorists" are those who organize, plan, and carry out terrorist activities or are members of any terrorist organizations.[12]

The Decision also provides the procedure for developing lists of terrorist organizations and terrorists: a leading State counterterrorism task force is to be established, which will decide on and adjust the lists, and such lists will then be published by the State Council public security department (i.e., the Ministry of Public Security).[13]

III. Domestic References to Extremism

Despite the fact that the concepts of extremism, terrorism, and separatism are defined by multilateral and bilateral treaties that China has entered into (discussed in Part IV of this report), definitions of these concepts have not been found in domestic legislation. A 2011 White Paper issued by the nongovernmental organization Human Rights in China (HRIC) discussing the impact of the Shanghai Cooperation Organization (SCO) on counterterrorism and human rights indicated that a clear and precise definition of "extremism," as well "terrorism" and "separatism," as referred to in the Shanghai Convention, does not exist domestically in China.[14]

---

[9] NPC, *supra* note 1.

[10] Shouquan Fabu: Quanguo Renda Changweihui Guanyu Jiaqiang Fankong Gongzuo Youguan Wenti de Jueding [Authorized Publication: Decision on Issues Related to Strengthening Counterterrorism Work] (Oct. 29, 2011), XINHUANET, http://news.xinhuanet.com/politics/2011-10/29/c_111132865.htm, *archived at* http://perma.cc/7DCW-VY59.

[11] *Id.* art. 2.

[12] *Id.*

[13] *Id.* art. 4.

[14] HRIC, COUNTER-TERRORISM AND HUMAN RIGHTS: THE IMPACT OF THE SHANGHAI COOPERATION ORGANIZATION 68 (Mar. 2011) (hereinafter HRIC White Paper), http://www.hrichina.org/sites/default/files/publication_pdfs/2011-hric-sco-whitepaper-full.pdf, *archived at* http://perma.cc/LJ84-W5K7.

A. Government Statements

Domestically, extremism is more a vague and politicized notion appearing in government instruments than a precisely defined legal term. In these instruments, extremism is always linked with terrorism and separatism, which are rhetorically expressed as the "Three Forces" of "ethnic separatist forces, violent terrorist forces, and religious extremist forces."[15] As indicated by the term "religious extremist forces," extremism is often found to be connected with religion.[16] The government statements say that the Three Forces are the same thing by nature, and have been colluding with each other from the very beginning to sabotage social stability.[17]

Furthermore, the Three Forces concept appears to be specifically applied to the groups of "East Turkestan" in the Xinjiang Uyghur Autonomous Region (XUAR) and "Free Tibet" in the Tibet Autonomous Region (TAR) (also translated as Xizang Autonomous Region).[18] This is consistent with the finding of the HRIC White Paper, which asserts that China has applied the concept of the "Three Evils" (the White Paper's terminology for the "Three Forces"[19]) in particular to the ethnic Uyghur population concentrated in the XUAR.[20]

The HRIC White Paper found that official Chinese government references to the Three Evils terminology appeared in a national development plan as early as March 15, 2001, prior to the establishment of the SCO in June of that year.[21] The White Paper states,

> [c]hapter 23 of the document, on "Rule by Law, Building a Socialist Country Governed According to Law," sets out the following priorities: "seriously study the new situations and new issues threatening social stability, correctly handle the inner conflicts among people during the new period, ensure social stability," and "crack down on ethnic splitting activities, *religious extremist* forces, violent terrorist activities, cults and illegal activities conducted in the name of religion."[22]

B. National Legislation

As discussed above, extremism is often connected with religion in government instruments. This is also true in the limited legislation containing this concept. The Regulation on Religious

---

[15] *See, e.g., He Wei Sangu Shili?* [*What Are the Three Forces?*], XINHUA (July 13, 2009), http://news.xinhuanet.com/politics/2009-07/13/content_11698031.htm, *archived at* http://perma.cc/4U7P-95KV.

[16] *Id.*

[17] *Id.*

[18] *See, e.g., Zhongguo Fei Chuantong Anquan de Liuda Tiaozhan Zhi Liu: Minzu Fenlie Zhuyi* [*The Sixth Challenge of the Six Untraditional State Security Challenges: Ethnic Separatism*], XINHUA (Aug. 10, 2004), http://news.xinhuanet.com/newscenter/2004-08/10/content_1751936.htm, *archived at* http://perma.cc/UVE4-K8RE.

[19] The HRIC White Paper refers to the "Three Forces" as the "Three Evils," and the approach of linking terrorism, separatism, and extremism as coequal targets as the "Three Evils Doctrine." HRIC White Paper, *supra* note 14, at 64.

[20] *Id.* at 64.

[21] *Id.* at 67.

[22] *Id.* (emphasis added).

Affairs expressly regulates extremism: when setting out the content that is prohibited from being published in religious publications, the Regulation includes "content which propagates *religious extremism*."[23] The Regulation does not provide a definition of "religious extremism," however.

Orders of the state radio, film, and television authority have banned content propagating religious extremism. The Regulation on Broadcasting and Television Administration prohibits radio and television stations from showing programs containing harmful content, including those "endangering the unity, sovereignty, and territorial integrity of the country," "endangering state security," and "instigating separation or disrupting ethnic solidarity."[24] Based on this provision, the State Administration of Radio Film and Television (SARFT) has expressly banned programs advocating religious extremism: pursuant to a SARFT order issued in 2010, television stations are prohibited from showing TV plays "opposing the state's religious policies, by advocating *religious extremism*, cults, and superstition; and by discriminating against or insulting religious beliefs."[25] Again, a definition of "religious extremism" is not provided by the SARFT order.

C. Local Legislation

At the local level, efforts at fighting against the Three Forces have particularly been found in the local regulations of the XUAR. The HRIC White Paper asserts that these regulations specific to the XUAR have become a key part of China's domestic counterterrorism legal framework.[26]

On December 29, 2009, the Standing Committee of the XUAR People's Congress amended the XUAR Regulation on the Comprehensive Management of Social Order. The amendments took effect on February 1, 2010.[27] The newly amended Regulation identifies acting against crimes endangering state security committed by "ethnic separatist forces, violent terrorist forces, and religious extremist forces" as one of the primary goals of managing social order in the XUAR.[28]

The TAR also has a set of provisions for managing social order, which emphasize fighting separatism. In the TAR Regulation on the Comprehensive Management of Social Order, acting against and preventing the crimes of separatism are among the primary goals of social order management in the autonomous region. Although the TAR Regulation includes provisions strengthening the management of religious activities and places, identifying such management as

---

[23] Zongjiao Shiwu Tiaoli [Regulation on Religious Affairs] (promulgated by the State Council on Nov. 30, 2004, effective Mar. 1, 2005), art. 7(4), LAWS AND REGULATIONS OF CHINA 3-289 (2009) (emphasis added).

[24] Guangbo Dianshi Guanli Tiaoli [Regulation on Broadcasting and Television Administration] (promulgated by the State Council, Aug. 11, 1997, effective Sept. 1, 1997), art. 32, LAWS AND REGULATIONS OF CHINA 3–369 (2009).

[25] Dianshiju Neirong Guanli Guiding [Provisions on the Administration of Contents of TV Plays] (issued by the SARFT, effective July 1, 2010), http://www.sarft.gov.cn/articles/2010/05/19/20100519184943720740.html (in Chinese; emphasis added), *archived at* http://perma.cc/F5YF-56JW.

[26] HRIC White Paper, *supra* note 14, at 72.

[27] Xinjiang Weiwuer Zizhiqu Shehui Zhi'an Zonghe Zhili Tiaoli [XUAR Regulation on the Comprehensive Management of Social Order] (promulgated Jan. 21, 1994, last amended Dec. 29, 2009, effective Feb. 1, 2010), http://news.ts.cn/content/2010-01/04/content_4685511.htm, *archived at* http://perma.cc/85B7-F4PH (click "Uploaded page").

[28] *Id.* art. 5(1).

a primary task, the words "religious extremism" or "terrorism" do not explicitly appear in the text.[29]

In addition, the XUAR promulgated a Regulation on Ethnic Unity Education on December 29, 2009, which includes "opposing ethnic separatist forces, violent terrorist forces, and religious extremist forces" as part of the primary content of ethnic unity education in the XUAR.[30]

IV. Extremism in Treaties

Extremism has been defined by the Shanghai Convention on Combating Terrorism, Separatism and Extremism (Shanghai Convention).[31]   According to the HRIC White Paper, the SCO approach to counterterrorism is actually modeled on the Three Evils (Three Forces) doctrine advanced by the Chinese government.[32]   The HRIC White Paper quotes the preamble of the Shanghai Convention, which says that the Three Evils are the focus of the Shanghai Convention and that the Convention "recognizes that these phenomena seriously threaten territorial integrity and security of the Parties as well as their political, economic and social stability."[33]

A. Extremism in the Shanghai Convention

"Extremism" is defined under the Shanghai Convention as

> an act aimed at seizing or keeping power through the use of violence or changing violently the constitutional regime of a State, as well as a violent encroachment upon public security, including organization, for the above purposes, of illegal armed formations and participation in them, criminally prosecuted in conformity with the national laws of the Parties.[34]

---

[29] Xizang Zizhiqu Shehui Zhi'an Zonghe Zhili Tiaoli [TAR Regulation on the Comprehensive Management of Social Order] (promulgated by the Standing Committee of the TAR People's Congress, last amended and effective June 6, 2007), *available at* the online Chinese law database, Chinalawinfo (Chinalawinfo Ref ID: 16935650).

[30] Xinjiang Weiwuer Zizhi Qu Minzu Tuanjie Jiaoyu Tiaoli [Regulation on Ethnic Unity Education] (effective Feb. 1, 2010), *available at* the Congressional-Executive Commission on China website, http://www.cecc.gov/pages/ virtualAcad/index.phpd?showsingle=135701 (last visited Dec. 12, 2012), *archived at* http://perma.cc/R734-BMHF.

[31] The Shanghai Convention was signed by the Republic of Kazakhstan, the People's Republic of China, the Kyrgyz Republic, the Russian Federation, the Republic of Tajikistan, and the Republic of Uzbekistan on June 15, 2001 in Shanghai, and entered into force on March 29, 2003. Shanghai Convention, June 15, 2001, available in English at http://www.unhcr.org/refworld/pdfid/49f5d9f92.pdf (last visited Dec. 12, 2012), *archived at* http://perma.cc/FY8A-UJUF. The NPC Standing Committee ratified the Convention on Oct. 27, 2001. Quanguo Renmin Daibiao Dahui Changwu Weiyuanhui Guanyu Pizhun Daji Kongbu Zhuyi, Fenlie Zhuyi he Jiduan Zhuyi Shanghai Gongyue de Jueding [NPC Standing Committee Decision on Ratifying Shanghai Convention on Combating Terrorism, Separatism and Extremism] (Oct. 27, 2001), NATIONAL PEOPLE'S CONGRESS, http://www.gov.cn/gongbao/ content/2001/content 61187.htm (last visited Dec. 12, 2012), *archived at* http://perma.cc/69S8-FJ6V (click "Uploaded page").

[32] HRIC White Paper, *supra* note 14, at 64.

[33] *Id.* at 41.

[34] Shanghai Convention art. 1(3).

The Shanghai Convention also defines "terrorism" and "separatism" as follows:

1) "terrorism" means:
   a. any act recognized as an offence in one of the treaties listed in the Annex to this Convention (hereinafter referred to as "the Annex") and as defined in this Treaty;
   b. other act [sic] intended to cause death or serious bodily injury to a civilian, or any other person not taking an active part in the hostilities in a situation of armed conflict or to cause major damage to any material facility, as well as to organize, plan, aid and abet such act, when the purpose of such act, by its nature or context, is to intimidate a population, violate public security or to compel public authorities or an international organization to do or to abstain from doing any act, and prosecuted in accordance with the national laws of the Parties;[35]
2) "separatism" means any act intended to violate territorial integrity of a State including by annexation of any part of its territory or to disintegrate a State, committed in a violent manner, as well as planning and preparing, and abetting such act, and subject to criminal prosecuting in accordance with the national laws of the Parties[.][36]

Parties to the Shanghai Convention have pledged to cooperate in the areas of prevention, identification, and suppression of terrorist, separatist, and extremist acts.[37] In their mutual relations, the parties consider these acts to be extraditable offenses.[38]

B. Bilateral Agreements on Combating Terrorism, Separatism, and Extremism

China has entered into bilateral agreements on combating terrorism, separatism, and extremism with members of the SCO, but not limited to these members. These agreements adopted the approach of the Shanghai Convention with regard to counterterrorism, to explicitly cover the elements of the Three Forces—terrorism, separatism, and extremism:

- Agreement Between the People's Republic of China and Kyrgyzstan on Cooperation in Combating Terrorism, Separatism, and Extremism (signed Dec. 11, 2002, effective Oct. 1, 2004).[39]

- Agreement Between the People's Republic of China and Kazakhstan on Cooperation in Combating Terrorism, Separatism, and Extremism (signed Dec. 23, 2002, effective July 3, 2003).[40]

---

[35] *Id.* art. 1(1).

[36] *Id.* art. 1(2).

[37] *Id.* art. 2.

[38] *Id.*

[39] DEPARTMENT OF TREATY OF LAW, MINISTRY OF FOREIGN AFFAIRS OF THE PEOPLE'S REPUBLIC OF CHINA, A COLLECTION OF TREATIES ON EXTRADITION AND AGREEMENTS ON COOPERATION IN COMBATING TERRORISM, SECESSIONISM AND EXTREMISM 874 (2009) (in Chinese).

[40] *Id.* at 898.

- Agreement Between the People's Republic of China and Tajikistan on Cooperation in Combating Terrorism, Separatism, and Extremism (signed Sept. 2, 2003, effective Feb. 7, 2006).[41]

- Agreement Between the People's Republic of China and Uzbekistan on Cooperation in Combating Terrorism, Separatism, and Extremism (signed Sept. 4, 2003, effective Oct. 21, 2004).[42]

- Agreement Between the People's Republic of China and Pakistan on Cooperation in Combating Terrorism, Separatism, and Extremism (signed Apr. 5, 2005, effective Dec. 12, 2006).[43]

- Agreement Between the People's Republic of China and Turkmenistan on Cooperation in Combating Terrorism, Separatism, and Extremism (signed Oct. 31, 2006, effective Feb. 6, 2007).[44]

- Agreement Between the People's Republic of China and Russian Federation on Cooperation in Combating Terrorism, Separatism, and Extremism (signed Sept. 27, 2010, effective Dec. 31, 2011).[45]

---

[41] *Id.* at 911.

[42] *Id.* at 931.

[43] *Id.* at 948.

[44] *Id.* at 966.

[45] Quanguo Renda Changweihui Guanyu Pizhun Zhonghua Renmin Gongheguo he Eluosi Lianbang Guanyu Daji Kongbu Zhuyi, Fenlie Zhuyi he Jiduan Zhuyi de Hezuo Xieding de Jueding [Decision of the Standing Committee of the National People's Congress on Ratifying the "Agreement between the People's Republic of China and the Russian Federation on Cooperation in Combating Terrorism, Separatism and Extremism"] (Dec. 31, 2011), NATIONAL PEOPLE'S CONGRESS, http://www.npc.gov.cn/npc/xinwen/2012-01/01/content_1685019.htm, *archived at* http://perma.cc/3RU5-E48N, text of the Agreement in Chinese, http://www.npc.gov.cn/wxzl/gongbao/2012-03/05/content_1705030.htm (last visited Dec. 12, 2012), *archived at* http://perma.cc/95CY-FZH8.

Pakistan

Tariq Ahmad
Legal Research Analyst[*]

SUMMARY   Pakistan has principally adopted an antiterrorism legal framework in order to address extremist activity in the country. Though Pakistan does not have a specific crime of "extremism" within its laws, it does have a series of other connected criminal offenses, primarily crimes against the state or incitement crimes, that form a close proximity to the crime of extremism defined under international conventions and statutes of other countries. Such provisions can be found in Pakistan's principal antiterrorism law, the Anti-terrorism Act, 1997, and in Pakistan's Penal Code. Pakistan's antiterrorism law is enforced through specialized antiterrorism courts and a listing system to designate organizations and individuals involved with terrorism. However, critics have called into question the effectiveness of the system to deal with terrorism.

More recently, however, Pakistan's legal approach to combating terrorism and extremism has become increasingly militarized, with the establishment of specialized military courts to try suspected terrorists.

Over the years Pakistan has also attempted, with little success, to regulate and reform the madrasa education system. Besides legal regulations, Pakistan has also attempted to institute programs promoting "antiradicalization" and sectarian harmony in the country.

I. Forms of 'Extremist' Challenges Faced by Pakistan

Pakistan faces a number of extremist challenges from both ethnic and religious groups in the country. According to Muhammad Amir Rana, Director of the Pakistan Institute of Peace Studies (PIPS), "[e]xtremism is defined in Pakistan in a number of ways, mainly in political, religious and social contexts. A lack of consensus even on definitions make [sic] it difficult to arrive at a comprehensive understanding of the phenomenon, further complicating efforts aimed at countering extremism."[1] According to PIPS researchers Abdul Basit and Mujtaba Rathore, however, "religious extremism is the common prevalent factor in all the visible trends and patterns of radicalization in Pakistan."[2]

Pakistan faces enormous challenges from extremist groups, particularly sectarian violence and terrorism perpetrated by radical Islamic groups. Some of the current challenges Pakistan faces in

---

[*] This report was last updated in September 2015.

[1] Muhammad Ameer Rana, Abstract, *Litterateurs' Response to Extremism in Pakistan*, 3 PIPS RES. J. CONFLICT & PEACE STUD. 112 (Apr.–June 2010), http://san-pips.com/index.php?action=journal&id=6, *archived at* http://perma.cc/L77J-V3XJ.

[2] Abdul Basit & Mujtaba Muhammmad Rathore, *Trends and Patterns of Radicalization in Pakistan*, 3 PIPS RES. J. CONFLICT & PEACE STUD. 16 (Apr.–June 2010).

respect to extremism can be traced to the "Islamization" policies of Pakistan's military leader General Zia-ul-Haq. According to a 2009 International Crisis Group report,

> Radical jihadi groups benefited from state patronage, for the first time, during General Zia-ul-Haq's military regime in the 1980s. They were backed for the twin purpose of fighting in the U.S.-supported anti-Soviet jihad in Afghanistan and promoting Sunni orthodoxy at home. That patronage continued even during the democratic interlude in the 1990s, as the military used its jihadi allies in India-administered Kashmir and in support of the Taliban in Afghanistan. As radical Sunni groups proliferated and grew stronger, sectarian violence became the primary source of terrorism in Pakistan.[3]

From 2001 to the present, Pakistan has been involved in military operations against tribal militancy in the northern regions of the country, including actions against various entities in Federally Administered Tribal Areas and separatist movements in the province of Baluchistan. Baluch ethno-nationalists and separatists have been waging a low-level insurgency for many years.[4] Sectarian and terrorist attacks on the Shia Hazara community has also "compounded the effects" of the "high-intensity conflict" between the separatists and the military.[5] Deobandi Sunni sectarian groups claim responsibility for most of the attacks against the Hazara Shias.[6]

Moreover, Pakistan's most populous city, Karachi, has witnessed some of the worst ethnic and sectarian violence in years, involving "sectarian militant groups, terrorist outfits, political parties, and criminal gangs."[7] The Pakistan military and other law enforcement agencies are currently involved in operations against militant and criminal elements in the city.[8] Therefore, some argue that extremist violence in the country is also motivated by ethnic and provincial divisions. As emphasized by Selig Harrison, Director of the Asia Program at the Center for International Policy,

> [a] single-minded focus [on terrorism] ignores a broader and more fundamental issue that cuts across the struggle between Islamist and secular forces: whether the multi-ethnic Pakistan federation, torn by growing tensions between a dominant Punjabi majority and

---

[3] INTERNATIONAL CRISIS GROUP, PAKISTAN: THE MILITANT JIHADI CHALLENGE 4 (Asia Report No. 164, Mar. 13, 2009), http://www.crisisgroup.org/~/media/Files/asia/south-asia/pakistan/164_pakistan___the_militant_jihadi_challenge.pdf, *archived at* http://perma.cc/4RFY-TB4T.

[4] *Bomb Blast at Hotel Kills 11 in Southwest Pakistan*, REUTERS AFRICA (Aug. 14, 2011), http://af.reuters.com/article/worldNews/idAFTRE77D0ZD20110814, *archived at* http://perma.cc/73TM-JBNZ.

[5] SAIRA YAMIN & SALMA MALIK, UNITED STATES INSTITUTE OF PEACE, MAPPING CONFLICT TRENDS IN PAKISTAN 3 (2014), http://www.usip.org/sites/default/files/PW93-Mapping_Conflict_Trends_in_Pakistan.pdf, *archived at* http://perma.cc/CDX2-LAKT.

[6] *Id.* at 12.

[7] *Id.* at 3; *see also Karachi Targeted Killings, Highest in 15 Years*, THE EXPRESS TRIBUNE (Oct. 29, 2010), http://tribune.com.pk/story/69491/karachi-target-killings-highest-in-15-years, *archived at* http://perma.cc/94P5-FDN9.

[8] Omar Hamid, *Military Intervention Has Reduced Terrorism Risks in Karachi But Allowed Pakistan's Military to Consolidate Influence Over Policy Direction*, IHS JANE'S 360 (Sept. 8, 2015), http://www.janes.com/article/54115/military-intervention-has-reduced-terrorism-risks-in-karachi-but-allowed-pakistan-s-military-to-consolidate-influence-over-policy-direction, *archived at* http://perma.cc/2M9S-FWHX.

increasingly disaffected Baluch, Sindhi and Pashtun ethnic minorities, can survive in its present form without basic political and economic reforms.[9]

II. System of National Laws Aimed at Fighting Extremism

Historically, Pakistan has principally adopted an "antiterrorism" legal framework in order to address extremist activity and sectarian violence in the country. In the context of increasing sectarian and political violence in Pakistan, the then Nawaz Sharif government promulgated the Anti-terrorism Act, 1997, establishing Pakistan's principal antiterrorism regime.[10] In the last few years Pakistan has passed a number of additional antiterrorism laws, including the National Counterterrorism Authority Act,[11] the Investigation for Fair Trial Act,[12] the Protection of Pakistan Act of 2014, and several amendments to the Anti-terrorism Act of 1997.[13]

In early July 2013, the Nawaz Sharif government unveiled a draft counterterrorism policy, which generally adopted the same strategy as the previous government to address militancy through five elements: dismantle, contain, prevent, educate, and reintegrate militants.[14]

In late December 2014, following the Peshawar school massacre, the Prime Minister announced a twenty-point National Action Plan to counter terrorism that included proposals to establish military courts to try alleged terrorists, strengthen NACTA, and counter hate speech and extremist material.[15] More recently, however, Pakistan's antiterrorism efforts have become increasingly militarized with the passage of the 21st Constitutional Amendment Act[16] and the Pakistan Army (Amendment) Act, 2015,[17] which provide the legal framework for establishing specialized military courts to try civilian terrorist suspects.

---

[9] SELIG S. HARRISON, PAKISTAN: THE STATE OF THE UNION 5 (Special Report, Center for Int'l Policy, Apr. 2009), http://www.ciponline.org/images/uploads/publications/pakistan_the_state_of_the_union.pdf, *archived at* http://perma.cc/A53U-967E.

[10] Anti-Terrorism Act, No. 27 of 1997, *available at* http://www.punjabcode.punjab.gov.pk/public/dr/THE%20 ANTI-TERRORISM%20ACT,%201997.doc.pdf, *archived at* http://perma.cc/F56K-4J24.

[11] National Counterterrorism Authority Act, No. 19 of 2013, http://www.na.gov.pk/uploads/documents/1364795170 _139.pdf, *archived at* http://perma.cc/FU2R-ZZES.

[12] Investigation for Fair Trial Act, No. 1 of 2013, http://www.na.gov.pk/uploads/documents/1361943916_947.pdf, *archived at* http://perma.cc/738F-G47D.

[13] Protection of Pakistan Act of 2014, No. 10 of 2014, http://www.na.gov.pk/uploads/documents/1409034186_ 281.pdf, *archived at* http://perma.cc/Y4NP-U8ML.

[14] Baqir Sajjad Syed, *No Radical Shift in New Anti-terror Strategy*, DAWN (July 6, 2013), http://www.dawn.com/ news/1023175, *archived at* http://perma.cc/9P96-ETFL; Irfan Ghauri, *Fighting Terror: Draft Policy Aims to Dismantle Terror Networks*, THE EXPRESS TRIBUNE (Aug. 13, 2013), http://tribune.com.pk/story/589497/fighting-terror-draft-policy-aims-to-dismantle-terror-networks, *archived at* http://perma.cc/4AUP-PCK3.

[15] Abdul Manan, *Fight Against Terrorism: Defining Moment*, THE EXPRESS TRIBUNE (Aug. 13, 2013), http://tribune.com.pk/story/811947/fight-against-terrorism-defining-moment, *archived at* http://perma.cc/A6Q6-HZTC.

[16] Constitution (Twenty-first Amendment) Act, No. 1 of 2015, http://www.na.gov.pk/uploads/documents/ 1420800195_264.pdf, *archived at* http://perma.cc/7XKF-QBEG.

[17] Pakistan Army (Amendment) Act, No. 2 of 2015, http://www.na.gov.pk/uploads/documents/1420800454_ 327.pdf, *archived at* http://perma.cc/PT9V-QUKU.

III. Crime of Extremism and Related Crimes

Pakistan does not have a specific crime of extremism within its laws. However, it does have a series of other criminal and terrorism-related offenses that form a close proximity to the crime of extremism as defined under international conventions and the statutes of other countries.

As noted above, Pakistan had adopted principally an antiterrorism legal framework in order to address extremist activity and sectarian violence in the country. Section 6 of Pakistan's Anti-terrorism Act defines "terrorism" to mean "the use or threat of action" where an action falls within certain stipulated acts and where

> [the] use or threat is designed to coerce and intimidate or overawe the Government or the public or a section of the public or community or sect or a foreign government or population or an international organization or create a sense of fear or insecurity in society; or

> The use or threat is made for the purpose of advancing a religious, sectarian or ethnic cause or intimidating and terrorizing the public, social sectors, media persons, business community or attacking the civilians, including damaging property by ransacking, looting, arson or by any other means, Government officials, installations, security forces or law enforcement agencies.

> Provided that nothing herein contained shall apply to a democratic and religious rally or a peaceful demonstration in accordance with law.[18]

Acts of terrorism are stipulated under section 6(2) of the Act and include, *inter alia*, acts committed by a person who "[i]ncites hatred and contempt on [a] religious, sectarian or ethnic basis to stir up violence or cause internal disturbance,"[19] or is involved in "dissemination, preaching ideas, teachings and beliefs as per [his/her] own interpretation on FM stations or through any other means of communication without explicit approval of the Government or its concerned departments."[20]

Section 8 of the Anti-terrorism Act, 1997, defines a separate crime that "prohibits acts intended to stir-up sectarian hatred." According to the Act,

> [a] person
> who:–
>   (a)   uses threatening, abusive or insulting words or behavior; or
>   (b)   displays, publishes or distributes any written material which is threatening, abusive or insulting: or words or behavior; or
>   (c)   distributes or shows or plays a recording or visual images or sounds which are threatening, abusive or insulting: or

---

[18] Anti-Terrorism Act, 1997, § 6(1)(b)–(c) (citations in original omitted).

[19] *Id.* § 6(2)(f).

[20] *Id.* § 6(2)(p).

(d) has in his possession written material or a recording or visual images or sounds which are threatening, abusive or insulting with a view to their being displayed or published by himself or another,

Shall be guilty of an offence if:–

 i. he intends thereby to stir up sectarian hatred; or

 ii. having regard to all the circumstances, sectarian hatred is likely to be stirred up thereby.[21]

The 1997 Act also criminalizes "printing, publishing, or disseminating any material" that "incites religious, sectarian or ethnic hatred."[22] However, to bring certain offenses within the ambit of the Anti-terrorism Act 1997, "it is essential to examine that the offence should have [a] nexus with the object of the Act"[23]—namely, creating terror, panic, or a sense of insecurity among the general public.[24]

Section 11X of the 1997 Act also prohibits the instigation of "civil commotion." According to the Act, "[a] person commits an offence if he makes any call for action or shut-down, imposed through the use of threats or force resulting in damage or destruction of property or injury to person, to intimidate citizens and prevent them from carrying out their lawful trade or business activity."[25]

Pakistan's Penal Code, under the title of "Offences Against the State," makes it a punishable offense to "wage war" against the state, and to conspire to do so.[26] Moreover, the statute also criminalizes conspiracies to "deprive Pakistan of the sovereignty of her territories or of any part thereof," or to "overawe, by means of criminal force or the show of criminal force, the Federal Government or any Provincial Government."[27] Under section 153-A of Pakistan's Penal Code, "promoting enmity between different groups" is a punishable criminal offense. The section stipulates that "no subject is entitled to write or say or do anything whereby the feelings of one class of subjects should be inflamed against another class of subjects."[28] According to the statute,

---

[21] *Id.* § 8.

[22] *Id.* § 11W.

[23] ISHFAQ ALI, ANTI-TERRORISM ACT, 1997: WITH ALL AMENDMENTS & UP-TO-DATE CASE LAWS 1 (Al-Noor Law Book House, 2008).

[24] *Id.* at 2.

[25] Anti-Terrorism Act, 1997, § 11X.

[26] PAK. PENAL CODE, 1860, §§ 121, 121-A, http://pakistancode.gov.pk/UY2FqaJw2-apaUY2Fqa-apk=-sg-jjjjjjjjjjjj-con-177, *archived at* http://perma.cc/74YG-ARH7.

[27] *Id.* § 121-A.

[28] SHAUKAT MAHMOOD & NADEEM SHAUKAT, THE PAKISTAN PENAL CODE: EXHAUSTIVE COMMENTARY INCORPORATING CASE-LAW OF PAKISTAN, BANGLADESH, BURMA, INDIA, U.K., ETC. 507 (Legal Research Centre, 2008).

[w]hoever,

(a) by words, either spoken or written, or by signs, or by visible representations or otherwise, promotes or incites, or attempts to promote or incite, on grounds of religion, race, place of both [sic], residence[,] language, caste or community or any other ground whatsoever, disharmony or feelings of enmity, hatred or ill-will between different religious, racial, language or regional groups or castes or communities; or

(b) commits, or incites any other person to commit, any act which is prejudicial to the maintenance of harmony between different religious, racial, language or regional groups or castes or communities or any group of persons identifiable as such on any ground whatsoever and which disturbs or is likely to disturb public tranquillity; or

(c) organizes, or incites any other person to organize, and exercise, movement, drill or other similar activity intending that the participants in any such activity shall use or be trained to use criminal force or violence or knowing it to be likely that the participants in any such activity will use or be trained to use criminal force or violence or participates, or incites any other person to participate, in any such activity intending to use or be trained to use criminal force or violence or knowing it to be likely that the participants in any such activity will use or be trained, to use criminal force or violence, against any religious, racial, language or regional group or caste of community or any group of persons identifiable as such on any ground whatsoever and any such activity for any reason whatsoever cause or is likely to cause fear or alarm or a feeling of insecurity amongst members of such religious, racial, language or regional group or caste or community[,] shall be punished with imprisonment for a term which may extend to five years and with [a] fine.[29]

The above section only applies where the hatred or enmity is created between different classes of people in Pakistan, not individuals within the same class. Essentially, it is a statutory provision "for the purpose of preserving order and amity between various classes of subjects."[30]

As indicated above, offences were also recently added to the Pakistan Army Act, 1952, so suspected terrorists "claiming or are known to belong to any terrorist group or organization using the name of religion or a sect"[31] can be tried by newly established military courts. Offenses include but are not limited to acts that "over-awe the state or any section of the public or sect or religious minority"[32] or "create terror or insecurity in Pakistan or attempt to commit any of the said acts within or outside Pakistan."[33]

---

[29] PAK. PENAL CODE, 1860, § 153-A.

[30] MAHMOOD & SHAUKAT, *supra* note 28, at 507.

[31] Pakistan Army (Amendment) Act, 2015, § 2, http://www.na.gov.pk/uploads/documents/1420547219_955.pdf, *archived at* http://perma.cc/M85V-8XE4.

[32] *Id.*

[33] *Id.*

IV. Enforcement and Effectiveness of Laws

A. Listing of Proscribed Organizations

Under section 11B of the Anti-terrorism Act, the federal government has the power to proscribe or list an organization if it has "reason to believe that an organization is concerned in terrorism." Section 11A stipulates that an organization is "concerned in terrorism" if it

> (a) commits[,] [facilitates] or participates in acts of terrorism; (b) prepares for terrorism; (c) promotes or encourages terrorism; (d) supports and assists any organization concerned with terrorism; (e) patronizes and assists in the incitement of hatred and contempt on religious, sectarian or ethnic lines that stir up disorder; (f) fails to expel from its ranks or ostracize those who commit acts of terrorism and presents them as heroic persons; or (g) is otherwise concerned in terrorism.[34]

Such organizations are listed under the First Schedule of the Act. Measures that may be taken against a proscribed organization include sealing its offices; and impounding all literature, posters, banners, and printed, electronic, digital, or other materials. The federal government may also ban the publication, printing, or distribution of any press statements, press conference, or public utterances by or on behalf of or in support of a proscribed organization.[35]

Organizations that the federal government believes may be concerned with terrorism can be put under an observation order pursuant to section 11D of the Act, and individuals who are concerned or suspected of being concerned with terrorism can also be listed.[36]

Critics have called into question the effectiveness of Pakistan's terrorist listing system. Some fault the lack of political will[37] and institutional capacity[38] in dealing with terrorist organizations effectively. One particular problem has been that proscribed organizations rebrand themselves with new names. In March 2013, Pakistan's Parliament enacted the Anti-Terrorism (Second Amendment) Act, 2013[39] to allow the government to deal with proscribed organizations that "form a new organization under a different name."[40] More recently, however, the head of the National Counter Terrorism Authority (NACTA) acknowledged the failure of the government to

---

[34] Anti-Terrorism Act, 1997, § 11A.

[35] *Id.* § 11E(1).

[36] *Id.* § 11D.

[37] INTERNATIONAL CRISIS GROUP, PAKISTAN: REVISITING COUNTER-TERRORISM STRATEGIES IN PAKISTAN: OPPORTUNITIES AND PITFALLS 8 (Asia Report No. 271, July 22, 2015), http://www.crisisgroup.org/~/media/Files/asia/south-asia/pakistan/271-revisiting-counter-terrorism-strategies-in-pakistan-opportunities-and-pitfalls.pdf, *archived at* http://perma.cc/Y9JT-NV5D.

[38] Ch. 2, *Country Reports: South and Central Asia Overview*, U.S. DEPARTMENT OF STATE, OFFICE OF THE COORDINATOR FOR COUNTERTERRORISM, COUNTRY REPORTS ON TERRORISM 2013, at 198 (Apr. 2014), http://www.state.gov/documents/organization/225886.pdf, *archived at* http://perma.cc/A5W2-GUQT.

[39] Anti-terrorism (Second Amendment) Act, 2013.

[40] *Id.* § 4.

renew actions against proscribed organizations and the lack of a procedure or mechanism to observe the activities of groups that have changed their names.[41]

Other recent statements are seen by some as demonstrating a lack of political will to effectively deal with militant organizations. A July 8, 2015, news article reported that the Minister for States and Frontier Regions said that there was no evidence that Jamaatud Dawa (JuD), which is regarded as the political or charitable wing of the banned militant group Lashkar-e-Taiba (LeT), was involved in terrorist activity. Instead, he reportedly said that the group was "under observation in terms of Section 11-D of the Anti-Terrorism Act since Nov. 15, 2003 and the provinces had been asked to keep a watch on its activities."[42]

On February 11, 2015, the Interior Minister of Pakistan announced efforts to reconcile the "national list" of proscribed organizations with those listed by the United Nations as being part of Al-Qaida, the Taliban, or associated groups.[43]

B. Prosecution and Trials of Suspected Terrorists

Under the Anti-terrorism Act, Pakistan has also established special, parallel antiterrorism courts known as ATCs. The purpose of the ATCs is to provide speedy trials for "heinous offences."[44] These Courts have jurisdiction over crimes stipulated under the Anti-terrorism Act. Moreover, some offenses that have "no apparent nexus with 'terrorism' may also be tried by an Anti-Terrorism Court" if such offenses are included in the Third Schedule of the Anti-terrorism Act.[45] Courts can be established by the federal or provincial governments. The ATC judges are appointed by the government and can be headed by a judge of a sessions court, an additional sessions judge, district magistrate, deputy district magistrate, or advocate with ten or more years of experience.[46] Decisions of the ATCs are appealable to the respective High Court, and the High Court's decision can then be appealed to the Supreme Court.

Pointing to a high acquittal rate,[47] critics have questioned the effectiveness of Pakistan's antiterrorism courts to adequately deal with terrorism. According to data compiled in 2012 by

---

[41] Azam Khan, *Not in the Short Term: Govt Quietly Dilutes Its Counter-terrorism Plan*, THE EXPRESS TRIBUNE (Mar. 8, 2015), http://tribune.com.pk/story/849724/not-in-the-short-term-govt-quietly-dilutes-its-counter-terrorism-plan, *archived at* http://perma.cc/J53R-JN5N.

[42] Iftikhar A. Khan, *No Evidence About JuD's Links with LeT: Minister*, DAWN (July 8, 2015), http://www.dawn.com/news/1193106/no-evidence-about-juds-links-with-let-minister, *archived at* http://perma.cc/3LZ6-TAZQ.

[43] Irfan Haider, *Pakistan's Banned Organisations List to Match UN Blacklist*, DAWN (Feb. 11, 2015), http://www.dawn.com/news/1162733, *archived at* http://perma.cc/JTD5-TRN6. For information on the UN terrorism listing system, *see* Security Council Committee Pursuant to Resolutions 1267 (1999) and 1989 (2011) Concerning Al-Qaida and Associated Individuals and Entities, https://www.un.org/sc/suborg/en/sanctions/1267 (scroll down to "Listing Criteria" at the bottom), *archived at* https://perma.cc/NF7F-JNSG.

[44] NATIONAL POLICE BUREAU ISLAMABAD, MANUAL ON ANTI-TERRORISM ACT, 1997, at 7 (Oct. 2008), *available at* https://www.unodc.org/tldb/pdf/Pakistan_Anti-terrorism_Manual_2008.pdf, *archived at* https://perma.cc/3S9Q-N9PF.

[45] *Id.* at 13.

[46] Anti-Terrorism Act, 1997, § 14.

[47] Ch. 2, *Country Reports: South and Central Asia Overview*, *supra* note 38, at 196.

the provincial government of Punjab, 75% of terrorism suspects arrested in the province over the last two decades were set free by antiterrorism courts.[48] According to a 2011 State Department report the national figure could be closer to 85%.[49] A December 2014 *Dawn* news report stated that the conviction rate in three ATCs operating in Pakistan's capitol of Islamabad and its sister city, Rawalpindi, "remained low"—of the 205 cases that were heard in the ATCs operating in Rawalpindi "there were convictions in less than ten," and in Islamabad there were no convictions.[50]

Scholars and analysts have pointed to a number of issues that broadly affect Pakistan's criminal justice system as being responsible for the high acquittal rate in terrorism-related cases. Critics first highlight what they see as the defective investigative process of Pakistan's law enforcement agencies. They argue that local police lack sufficient skill and training in collecting evidence and also lack forensic and other modern investigative tools, which has made the investigation process ineffective in Pakistan. Analysts further state that, since investigating officers are unable to collect adequate evidence, prosecutors cannot build strong enough cases against suspected perpetrators. They also point out that ATCs are severely understaffed, underfunded, and lack essential resources. Furthermore, the non-appointment of ATC judges in the past has also been a substantial issue. Judgeship vacancies lead to huge backlogs of cases. Policy analyst Huma Yusuf has summarized these issues, observing in 2010 that

> [m]any of these problems stem from the fact that the government has not allotted enough funds for the ATC infrastructure, a problem that plagues the Pakistani legal system at large. Moreover, since they work for a parallel system, state prosecutors employed by ATCs cannot even utilize the scant resources available to the regular session courts. As a result, ATCs have failed to deliver on their primary mandate—quick justice.[51]

In addition, ATC trials are often delayed due to security concerns. Some scholars have noted that in cases where suspects are "accused of heinous crimes, in-camera trials are conducted in jail."[52] Moreover, "[a]rranging logistics for such hearings can lead to prolonged delays."[53]

---

[48] Asad Kharal, *Flawed Anti-terrorism Strategy: 75% Terror Suspects Set Free in Punjab*, THE EXPRESS TRIBUNE (Oct. 17, 2011), http://tribune.com.pk/story/275661/flawed-anti-terrorism-strategy-75-terror-suspects-set-free-in-punjab, *archived at* http://perma.cc/Z73E-JZXB. According to the Express Tribune report, "[s]ince 1990, there have been close to 800 incidents of terrorism in Punjab, of which 475 have actually been prosecuted. A total of 2,300 suspects were named in those cases, and about 2,200 arrested. Of those arrested, about 1,650 — or 75% — were acquitted by the courts due to a lack of evidence against them." *Id. See also* Malik Asad, *High Ratio of Acquittal: Punjab to Review ATC Prosecutors' Working*, DAWN (Dec. 9, 2012), http://www.dawn.com/news/770169/high-ratio-of-acquittal-punjab-to-review-atc-prosecutors-working, *archived at* http://perma.cc/XC56-M8S2.

[49] Ch. 2, *Country Reports: South and Central Asia Overview*, U.S. DEPARTMENT OF STATE, OFFICE OF THE COORDINATOR FOR COUNTERTERRORISM, COUNTRY REPORTS ON TERRORISM 2011, at 142 (July 2012), http://www.state.gov/documents/organization/195768.pdf, *archived at* http://perma.cc/XC56-M8S2.

[50] *Conviction Rate Slow in Anti-terrorism Courts in Pindi, Islamabad*, DAWN (Dec. 18, 2014), http://www.dawn.com/news/1151583, *archived at* http://perma.cc/R43L-JHAN.

[51] Huma Yusuf, *Pakistan's Anti-Terrorism Courts*, CTC SENTINEL (Mar. 3, 2010), https://www.ctc.usma.edu/posts/pakistan%E2%80%99s-anti-terrorism-courts, *archived at* https://perma.cc/UF8P-X2C6.

[52] *Id.*

[53] *Id.*

According to Huma Yusuf, "security concerns on the part of judges, state prosecutors, and defense counsels regularly lead to the postponement of hearings."[54] In addition, Pakistan lacks an adequate witness protection program, and complainants and witnesses often refuse to testify against the accused or turn hostile. In 2013, the province of Sindh enacted a witness protection law, but as of August 2014 news reports stated that the government had failed to enforce it.[55]

Concern also exists over the absence of any mechanism to monitor released suspected terrorists who have been acquitted or released on bail. Some have called for the "need to introduce new and scientific methods to keep strict checks on suspected terrorists even after their release upon bail or through acquittal."[56]

In an attempt to address some of these concerns, the Actions (in Aid of Civil Power) Regulation, 2011,[57] establishes a legal framework that "provides for detainee transfer to civilian custody for potential prosecution under Pakistan's criminal law."[58] Specialized courts have also been established to try persons who have committed certain scheduled offenses under the recently passed Protection of Pakistan Act, 2014.[59]

More recently, in response to the 2014 Peshawar school massacre, the government of Pakistan has established specialized military courts to try terrorism suspects. On January 6, 2015, the Parliament of Pakistan passed the 21st Constitutional Amendment Act and the Pakistan Army (Amendment) Act, 2015, "aimed to set up constitutionally protected military courts to try civilian terrorism suspects" for a two-year sunset period.[60] These Courts were reportedly established to deal with the ineffectiveness of Pakistan's criminal justice system to deal with terrorism-related cases. According to the Pakistan Army (Amendment) Act, they are meant for the "prevention of acts threatening the security of Pakistan by any terrorist group, armed group, wing and militia or their members using name of religion or a sect."[61] However, human rights organizations have questioned the independence and impartiality of what they see as a secret court system and have also raised concerns about the adequacy of fair trial protections that the trial processes provide.[62]

---

[54] *Id.*

[55] *Prosecution Suffers as Sindh Fails to Enforce Witness Protection Law*, DAWN (Aug. 2, 2014), http://www.dawn.com/news/1122442, *archived at* http://perma.cc/8KTW-KCSR.

[56] Anti-Terrorism (Second Amendment) Bill 2013, Analysis of § 11E1a(a)-(c), PILDAT LEGISLATIVE BRIEF, No. 18, at 2 (Feb. 2013), http://www.pildat.org/Publications/publication/Democracy&LegStr/PILDATLegislativeBrief18_AntiTerrorism2ndAmendmentBill_2013.pdf, *archived at* http://perma.cc/XXA7-XPJ4.

[57] Actions (in Aid of Civil Power) Regulation, 2011, *available at* http://www.isj.org.pk/the-actions-in-aid-of-civil-power-regulation-2011, *archived at* http://perma.cc/X2JP-98KG.

[58] Ch. 2, *Country Reports: South and Central Asia Overview*, *supra* note 38, at 142.

[59] Protection of Pakistan Act, 2014, § 8.

[60] *Parliament Passes 21st Constitutional Amendment, Army Act Amendment*, DAWN (Jan. 6, 2015), http://www.dawn.com/news/1155271, *archived at* http://perma.cc/82FE-Z46Z.

[61] Pakistan Army (Amendment) Act, preamble.

[62] Saroop Ijaz, *Dispatches: Pakistan's Military Courts Mistake*, HUMAN RIGHTS WATCH, (Aug. 6, 2015), https://www.hrw.org/news/2015/08/06/dispatches-pakistans-military-courts-mistake, *archived at* https://perma.cc/3DTA-8FWA; *see also* INTERNATIONAL COMMISSION OF JURISTS, PAKISTAN: MILITARY TRIALS

V. Madrassas and Education Reform

Madrassas (Islamic schools) were originally registered under the Societies Registration Act of 1860 but in 1996 a ban was imposed on such registrations.[63] This lead to the proliferation of unregulated madrassas in the country.

The madrassa reform process, which is seen as largely having stalled, was initiated in 2001 by then military leader and President Pervez Musharraf. In 2001, Musharraf promulgated the Pakistan Madrassa Education (Establishment and Affiliation of Model Dini Madaris) Board Ordinance which "created the Pakistan Madrassah Education Board with the responsibility of establishing new, exemplary *dini madaris*[64] (religious schools or colleges) and *darul uloom* ("houses of knowledge" or Islamic seminaries) and overseeing those dini madaris and darul uloom[65] that choose to affiliate with the Board."[66] The aim of the model dini madaris were to "demonstrate to existing madaris how to modernize and to train a new generation of liberal-minded ulema [religious scholars]."[67] A second ordinance was promulgated in June 2002, known as the Dini Madaris (Regulation and Control) Ordinance, which allowed madrassas to register on a voluntary basis to make regular financial declarations to the government; however, fierce opposition from the ulema prevented the latter ordinance from being fully implemented.[68] To date, only "three model madrassas (teaching modern subjects such as computing alongside religious subjects) have been established—two in Sindh and one in Islamabad."[69]

In 2005 the Societies Registration Act of 1860[70] was amended to require madrassas to register and to provide audit reports and a list of funding sources. However, the Ittehad-e-Tanzimat-e-Madaris-e-Dinya (ITMD), an umbrella organization of madrasas, rejected the amendments and refused to cooperate. According to a report by the Norwegian Peacebuilding Resource Centre (NOREF), "madrasas saw these measures as an attempt to assert stronger government control

---

FOR CIVILIANS QUESTIONS AND ANSWERS (Apr. 2015), http://icj.wpengine.netdna-cdn.com/wp-content/uploads/2015/04/Pakistan-Q-and-A-Military-Courts-Advocacy-Analysis-Brief-2015-ENG.pdf, *archived at* http://perma.cc/Y454-MMCJ.

[63] Testimony of Samina Ahmed, International Crisis Group, Before the U.S. Senate Foreign Relations Committee (Apr. 19, 2005), http://www.crisisgroup.org/en/publication-type/speeches/2005/testimony-of-samina-ahmed-to-us-senate-foreign-relations-committee.aspx, *archived at* http://perma.cc/2KFE-3983.

[64] "Madaris" is the plural form of "madrasa." The word can also be transliterated as *madrasah, madarasaa, medresa, madrassa, madraza, medrese*.

[65] The term can also be transliterated as *dar al-`ulum, darul ulum*, etc.

[66] Christopher Candland, *Pakistan's Recent Experience in Reforming Islamic Education, in* ROBERT M. HATHAWAY, EDUCATION REFORM IN PAKISTAN: BUILDING FOR THE FUTURE 155 (2005), http://academics.wellesley.edu/Polisci/Candland/MadarisReform.pdf, *archived at* http://perma.cc/25B8-S6DG.

[67] *Id.*

[68] *Id.*

[69] Humaira Israr, *Curbing Militancy: Regulating Pakistan's Madrassas*, INTERNATIONAL RELATIONS AND SECURITY NETWORK (ISN) (Sept. 18, 2015), http://www.isn.ethz.ch/Digital-Library/Articles/Detail/?lng=en&id=193401, *archived at* http://perma.cc/Z7LT-67PE.

[70] Societies Registration Act, No. 21 of 1860, http://www.mca.gov.in/Ministry/actsbills/pdf/Societies_Registration_Act_1860.pdf, *archived at* http://perma.cc/9FXF-HHDX.

over the madrasas and as a threat to the independence of the institutions."[71] Though the madrassas were willing to provide the government with audit reports, they rejected the government's requirement of providing "information on individual contributions."[72]

Eventually negotiations between the government and the madrassas resulted in another amendment to the Societies Registration Act. According to the 2007 amendment, madrassas must "sign a declaration stating that they shall not teach or publish any literature that promotes militancy or spreads sectarianism. They are also required to submit regular financial reports."[73] In return, the government must compromise on two demands from the ITMD: "(1) the madrasas that were already registered did not have to comply with the new reporting requirements and (2) financial reports did not have to reveal the madrasas' funding sources."[74] Another issue noted by the ICG is that the audit reports are "prepared by madrasas' chosen auditors without any independent inspection."[75]

In April 2014, the Government of Pakistan released a National Internal Security Policy, which noted the role of certain madrassas as a vehicle for spreading extremism. The policy stated that "troublesome aspects of these *madrassas*, which impinge on national internal security, include financing from unidentified sources [and the] publication and distribution of hate material."[76] The Policy calls for comprehensive madrassa reforms, and envisages, among other things, bringing all 22,000 madrassas in the country under the national education system within one year, and "supporting their administration, financial audit and curriculum accreditation."[77]

After the 2014 Peshawar school attack, the government, as part of its National Action Plan (NAP), called for steps to reform Pakistan's madrassa system, with a particular emphasis on registration and control of foreign funding. However, the ITMD has fiercely resisted these steps and has called on the government to honor previous agreements on madrassa reform.[78] More

---

[71] NOREF, Kaja Borchgrevink, Pakistan's Madrasas: Moderation or Militancy? The Madrasa Debate and the Reform Process 9 (June 2011), http://www.peacebuilding.no/var/ezflow_site/storage/original/application/d6f77e0632a20fcf1ae1ad65041acdc7.pdf, *archived at* http://perma.cc/U75K-DZ5W.

[72] *Id.*

[73] Kaja Borchgrevink, *Taking Stock: Madrasa Reform in Pakistan*, NOREF Policy Brief No. 4 at 5 (July 2011), http://www.peacebuilding.no/var/ezflow_site/storage/original/application/3308ff0d3c05ddf15eeda001676f27c8.pdf, *archived at* http://perma.cc/8XMU-BBYU.

[74] *Id.*

[75] International Crisis Group, Pakistan: Karachi's Madrasas And Violent Extremism 19 (Asia Report No. 130, Mar. 29, 2007), http://www.crisisgroup.org/~/media/Files/asia/south-asia/pakistan/130_pakistan_karachi_s_madrasas_and_violent_extremism.ashx, *archived at* http://perma.cc/D9V5-UEHC.

[76] Asad Hashim, *Pakistan Mulls Tighter Controls on Madrassas*, Al–Jazeera (Apr. 21, 2014), http://www.al jazeera.com/indepth/features/2014/04/pakistan-tighter-controls-madrassas-islamabad-201442064231355458.html, *archived at* http://perma.cc/H52R-229Q.

[77] *Id.*

[78] Imran Mukhtar, *Deadlock Persists on Madrassa Reforms*, The Nation (Feb. 22, 2015), http://nation.com.pk/national/22-Feb-2015/deadlock-persists-on-madrassa-reforms, *archived at* http://perma.cc/8YGD-YWKH; *'Stop Harassing Clerics, Identify Those Involved in Terrorist Activities,'* The Express Tribune (Mar. 2, 2015), http://tribune.com.pk/story/846350/stop-harassing-clerics-identify-those-involved-in-terrorist-activities, *archived at* http://perma.cc/F82P-JNXA; Noor Aftab, *ITMD Accuses Government of Launching Crackdown on Madrassas*, The

recently, however, the ITMD and the government have appeared to come to some agreement to finalize a form for registration, submit audit reports, create a mechanism for monitoring foreign funding with the cooperation of the State Bank of Pakistan, and implement curriculum reform.[79]

VI. Government Responses, Legislative Initiatives, and Preventive Measures

A. National Counter Terrorism Authority

Pakistan has continued to face challenges in regard to interagency cooperation and coordination on counterterrorism. In the last few years, however, it appears Pakistan has made efforts to "centralize coordination and information sharing."[80]

In December 2009, the Pakistani government formally established the National Counter Terrorism Authority (NACTA), a focal body mandated to coordinate national counterterrorism efforts and strategy. Because the body initially operated under the Interior Ministry it was criticized for lacking independence and was effectively downgraded to a governmental department rather than "the status of the country's supposedly premier counterterrorism organization."[81] In 2010, the head of NACTA resigned over efforts to try to bring the body under the direct chairmanship of the Prime Minister. Over the years, the body has largely laid dormant due to this bureaucratic in-fighting over whether NACTA should operate under the Prime Minister or the Interior Ministry.[82] In 2013 Pakistan's National Parliament passed the National Counter Terrorism Authority Act (NACTA Act),[83] giving the body formal statutory status and independence.

NACTA is mandated to "unify and orchestrate national counter-terrorism and counter-extremism measures"[84] that are already being implemented by several existing organizations. It is also tasked with "present[ing] strategic policy options to the government to be considered and

---

NEWS (Mar. 6, 2015), http://www.thenews.com.pk/Todays-News-6-305290-ITMD-accuses-government-of-launching-cr, *archived at* http://perma.cc/697S-MP6L (click "Uploaded page").

[79] Mian Abrar, *With Army Chief on Table, PM Brings Clergy on Board*, PAKISTAN TODAY (Sept. 8, 2015), http://www.pakistantoday.com.pk/2015/09/08/national/with-army-chief-on-table-pm-brings-clergy-on-board, *archived at* http://perma.cc/YL4V-4RDD (click "Uploaded page"); *Madrassas Agree on Funds Through Banks*, THE NATION (Sept. 8, 2015), http://nation.com.pk/editors-picks/08-Sep-2015/madrasas-agree-on-funds-thru-banks, *archived at* http://perma.cc/T9KB-5RJQ.

[80] *Pakistan Lost 1500 Lives to Terrorism in 2013: Taking Counterterror Steps: US Report*, AAJ.TV (May 1, 2015), http://www.aaj.tv/2014/05/pakistan-lost-1500-lives-to-terrorism-in-2013-taking-counterterror-steps-us-report, *archived at* http://perma.cc/47ST-5EBG.

[81] Zahid Hussain, *Nacta: A Non-starter*, DAWN.COM (Dec. 4, 2012), http://www.dawn.com/news/768693/nacta-a-non-starter, *archived at* http://perma.cc/CK4A-HG4Y.

[82] SHUJA NAWAZ, UNITED STATES INSTITUTE OF PEACE, WHO CONTROLS PAKISTAN'S SECURITY FORCES? (Special Report 5, Dec. 2011), http://www.usip.org/sites/default/files/SR%20297.pdf, *archived at* http://perma.cc/J28R-YEB9.

[83] National Counter Terrorism Authority Act, No. 19 of 2013, http://www.na.gov.pk/uploads/documents/1364795170_139.pdf, *archived at* http://perma.cc/AN5M-XG5B.

[84] Raja Asghar, *Anti-terror Law Adopted to Mark Women's Day*, DAWN (Mar. 9, 2013), http://www.dawn.com/news/791289/anti-terror-law-adopted-to-mark-womens-day, *archived at* http://perma.cc/9LBC-FKBE.

implemented by stakeholders,"[85] and is responsible for conducting scientific studies on extremism and terrorism. The authority is a focal point for the receipt of information and intelligence, and for the dissemination of data to relevant stakeholders in order to "formulate threat assessments with periodical reviews to be presented to the federal government for making adequate and timely efforts to counter terrorism and extremism."[86]

NACTA is governed by a Board of Governors, headed by the Prime Minister, and also includes a number of federal and provincial ministers including the Interior, Defense, and Finance ministers, and heads of law enforcement and intelligence agencies, including Inter-Services Intelligence, the Intelligence Bureau, Military Intelligence, and the Federal Investigation Agency. The NACTA Act also establishes the position of national coordinator to help execute "board-approved policies and plans."[87] The authority is assisted by an executive committee headed by the Interior Minister, and a national coordinator and deputy will execute the board's policies and the government's instructions. NACTA is also responsible for conducting scientific studies on extremism and terrorism.[88]

Despite the legislative efforts to revive NACTA, some critics feel the body still lacks capacity and remains largely inoperative, while others feel that the mandate of the body is far too "ambitious in its aims and scope,"[89] according to news reports. Nevertheless, under a February 2014 national security policy the government hopes to revive the body.[90]

After the December Peshawar School attack, the federal government announced its plans to activate and strengthen NACTA as part of the National Action Plan (NAP). However, it appears that the Joint Intelligence Directorate, which is meant to be set up under NACTA, still faces a shortage of funds.[91] In early June 2015, news sources reported that how the budget will be allocated for NACTA is still in dispute and that the government has failed to establish the Joint Intelligence Directorate.[92]

---

[85] *Pakistan Parliament Passes Counter-terrorism Authority Bill*, THE ECONOMIC TIMES (Mar. 9, 2013), http://articles.economictimes.indiatimes.com/2013-03-09/news/37581295_1_counter-terrorism-efforts-extremism-pakistan-parliament, *archived at* http://perma.cc/T3LA-V7M9.

[86] *Id.*

[87] *Counter-terrorism Authority Bill Moved in National Assembly*, DAWN (Feb. 1, 2013), http://www.dawn.com/news/782699/counter-terrorism-authority-bill-moved-in-national-assembly, *archived at* http://perma.cc/AN2Y-CD5Z.

[88] *Pakistan Parliament Passes Counter-terrorism Authority Bill*, *supra* note 85.

[89] Owais Arshad, *Pakistan's New National Security Policy*, MUFTAH (Mar. 9, 2014), http://muftah.org/national-security-policy/#.U15YMRBnGmQ, *archived at* http://perma.cc/Q5ZC-DZ5S.

[90] *Id.*

[91] Imran Mukhtar, *Joint Intelligence Directorate Still a Dream*, THE NATION (Mar. 18, 2015), http://nation.com.pk/national/18-Mar-2015/joint-intelligence-directorate-still-a-dream, *archived at* http://perma.cc/CBF2-GM2F.

[92] Azam Khan, *Billions for Counter-terrorism, Nothing for Nacta*, THE EXPRESS TRIBUNE (June 7, 2015), http://tribune.com.pk/story/899257/billions-for-counter-terrorism-nothing-for-nacta, *archived at* http://perma.cc/PTM3-PUMJ.

B. Sectarian Harmony

The government of Pakistan, under the auspices of the late Federal Minister for Minorities Affairs Shahbaz Bhatti, established local-level committees to promote religious tolerance and sectarian harmony. In July 2010, the Bhatti also announced the formation of "a National Interfaith Council aimed at promoting brotherhood, harmony and co-existence among various sects and faiths."[93]

C. Deradicalization Programs

The Pakistani Army runs a number of deradicalization centers for militants who were detained during the conflict in the Swat Valley. The goal of these programs is "to ideologically cleanse the inmates of the Taliban's radical teachings and to give them education and vocational skills so they can be employed once rehabilitated."[94] Moreover, "[c]orrective religious education is an essential part of the de-radicalization programs."[95] One such initiative is the Mishal, an Army-established deradicalization and rehabilitation facility for adult men who previously joined the Taliban.[96]

In 2009, the Pakistani Army initiated a youth deradicalization program in the Swat Valley through a rehabilitation center known as Sabawoon. The administration of the program was later transferred to a local nongovernmental organization, Hum Pakistani Foundation, and is funded by UNICEF. The program includes courses in secondary education and vocational training, and provides psychiatric counseling. The program also seeks to counter ideological beliefs that lead to extremism and terrorism through "corrective religious instruction."[97] As of 2014, the program claimed to have reintegrated over 2,200 youths.[98]

In August 2011, the Defence Committee of the Government Cabinet announced the possibility of a national deradicalization program aimed at combating rising extremism in the country. According to the Committee, "[i]t was decided in the committee that special attention shall be given to a de-radicalisation programme to motivate youth to engage and isolate them from

---

[93] *Bhatti Announces Setting up of National Interfaith Council*, ASSOCIATED PRESS OF PAKISTAN (July 12, 2010), http://www.app.com.pk/en /index.php?option=com content&task=view&id=109004&Itemid=2, *archived at* http://perma.cc/Y9R7-FQR8.

[94] Shehzad H. Qazi, *De-radicalizing the Pakistani Taliban*, HUFFPOST RELIGION (Oct. 4, 2011, 5:12 AM), http://www.huffingtonpost.com/shehzad-h-qazi/de-radicalizing-the-pakistani-taliban b 993208.html, *archived at* http://perma.cc/8D6U-HFT8.

[95] *Id.*

[96] *Id.*

[97] UNITED INSTITUTE OF PEACE, THE CHALLENGES OF COUNTERING RADICALIZATION IN PAKISTAN (May 9, 2012), http://www.usip.org/publications/the-challenges-countering-radicalization-in-pakistan, *archived at* http://perma.cc/3MB7-PR8F.

[98] Dr. Fawad Kaiser, *Swat Deradicalisation Project — I*, THE DAILY TIMES (Jan. 20, 2014), http://www.dailytimes.com.pk/opinion/20-Jan-2014/swat-deradicalisation-project-i, *archived at* http://perma.cc/HL8E-Q2JG.

militancy and terrorism and bring them back to peaceful living."[99] Moreover, Pakistan's Prime Minister, who presided over the meeting, stated,

> [w]e need to clearly identify the threat posed by terrorism, including the underlying factors such as ideological, motivational, funding, weapon supply, training and organizational support for terrorist groups and those aiding and abetting the terrorists.[100]

Policy analysts note the need for these programs to be "consolidated into an overall program in order to improve effectiveness, expand the participation, and increase international funding."[101] More recently in a national security policy paper, the government of Pakistan tasked NACTA, in consultation with other institutions, to develop a national deradicalization program to counter terrorism and extremism. The policy states that NACTA "will facilitate a dialogue with all stakeholders to strengthen democratic values of tolerance" and help create "a national narrative on extremism, terrorism, sectarianism and militancy . . . to dispel the wrong perceptions created by the terrorists on ideological basis."[102] The program will target persons, like youth, who are particularly vulnerable to extremism and will incorporate methods of rehabilitation and reintegration in society.

---

[99] Baqir Sajjad Syed, *'De-Radicalisation' Plan Under Study*, DAWN (Aug. 18, 2011), http://www.dawn.com/2011/08/18/de-radicalisation-plan-under-study.html, *archived at* http://perma.cc/4YVM-E53F.

[100] *Id.*

[101] INTERNATIONAL CENTRE FOR POLITICAL VIOLENCE AND TERRORISM RESEARCH, 1ST STRATEGIC WORKSHOP ON REHABILITATION AND DE-RADICALIZATION OF MILITANTS AND EXTREMISTS: REPORT ON A WORKSHOP ORGANISED BY THE FATA SECRETARIAT CAPACITY BUILDING PROJECT, May 18–19, 2010, p. 29, https://www.rsis.edu.sg/wp-content/uploads/2015/04/Report-1st-Strategic-Workshop-on-Rehabilitation-and-De-Radicalization-of-Militants-and-Extremist.pdf, *archived at* https://perma.cc/8XHU-ATC7.

[102] *Nacta to Develop Deradicalisation Programme*, THE NATION (Apr. 7, 2014), http://www.nation.com.pk/islamabad/07-Apr-2014/nacta-to-develop-deradicalisation-programme, *archived at* http://perma.cc/8DEX-RSHQ; *Internal Security Policy Aims for Deradicalisation in Pakistan*, THE HINDU (Mar. 2, 2014), http://www.thehindu.com/news/international/south-asia/internal-security-policy-aims-for-deradicalisation-in-pakistan/article5743530.ecev, *archived at* http://perma.cc/GAP7-CWBB.

Russia

Peter Roudik
*Director of Global Legal Research Directorate**

SUMMARY   The line between a hate crime and protected speech is not definitively established in the Russian Federation. Federal law subjects to prosecution perpetrators of violent and nonviolent forms of extremism as these acts are defined by the Criminal Code, Code of Administrative Violations, and framework Law on Countering Extremist Activity. The presence of a prejudicial motive appears to be a key factor in determining the extremist nature of an act, and if such a motivation is proven it is considered an aggravating circumstance. Both individuals and organizations can be found responsible for extremism. Prosecution of extremist crimes is usually based on conclusions of experts who decide on the presence of an extremist component in the actions charged. Information on materials deemed to be extremist is collected and published by the Ministry of Justice. These materials are prohibited from being made publicly accessible. Involvement in extremist activities is a reason for the state to impose restrictions on one's political or professional activities, or to liquidate an organization whose leaders have been accused of extremism. Reportedly, these provisions are often used by the government to silence the opposition, and the authorities have been criticized for focusing on minor crimes. In the summer of 2011, the Russian government identified the prevention of extremism as its major task, and an interagency commission on the subject has been established.

This report analyzes Russian anti-extremist legislation and reviews the procedural aspects of its application.

I. Constitutional Principles of Anti-Extremist Legislation

The Russian Constitution guarantees basic human rights, including freedom of speech, expression, and association. At the same time, it prohibits public associations that are aimed at forcibly changing the fundamental principles of the constitutional system and violating the integrity of the Russian Federation; undermining its security; setting up armed units; and instigating social, racial, national, and religious strife.[1] Also, propaganda promoting social, racial, national, or religious enmity or the instigation of such enmity, as well as propaganda promoting social, racial, national, religious or linguistic supremacy,[2] are prohibited. The term "extremism" is not used in the Constitution, however.

These restrictions appear to be in accordance with a constitutional provision (art. 55, para. 3) that allows the restriction of individuals' rights and freedoms by federal legislation to the extent necessary for the protection of fundamental principles of the constitutional system, morality,

---

* This report was last updated in April 2014. Foreign law consultants Nerses Isajanyan and Svitlana Vodyanyk contributed to the report.

[1] KONSTITUTSIIA ROSSIISKOI FEDERATSII [KONST. RF] [CONSTITUTION OF THE RUSSIAN FEDERATION], adopted Dec. 12, 1991, art. 13, para. 5.

[2] *Id.* art. 29, para. 2.

health, the rights and lawful interests of other people, and ensuring the defense of the country and the security of the state.[3] These restrictions appear to follow international standards elaborated by the European Court of Human Rights and other international and national authorities, which generally uphold restrictions on free expression on the grounds of national security where it can be shown that they are absolutely necessary in a democratic society, i.e., where the expression is intended to incite violence and there is a direct and immediate connection between the expression and the likelihood or occurrence of such violence.[4]

Although the federal government has exclusive jurisdiction in regulating the rights and freedoms of individuals and citizens, several constituent components of the Russian Federation have enacted legislation aimed at regulating freedom of conscience and religion.[5] While criminal law is within the exclusive jurisdiction of the federal government, these legal acts impose administrative responsibility for activities deemed to be in violation of the public order. For example, anti-extremist legislation was enacted in the Kabardino-Balkar Republic of the Northern Caucasus. This provincial law restricts proselytism and prohibits, among others things, religious organizations if the doctrine threatens public security and the lawful interests of citizens, or advocates the superiority of one religious doctrine over another.[6]

During the last two years, members of the Russian legislature several times proposed to amend the country's Constitution. Presently, the Constitution states that Russia is a secular state. In order to stress the exceptional role of the Orthodox faith, State Duma members Sergey Baburin and Elena Mizulina suggested the addition of a new article to the Constitution providing that "Orthodoxy shall be the basis of the national and cultural identity of Russia."[7]

II. Overview of Russian Anti-Extremist Legislation

The anti-extremist legislation of Russia consists of the Federal Law on Countering Extremist Activity[8] (Extremism Law), specific provisions of the Russian Federation Criminal Code,[9] the

---

[3] Aleksandr Sigarev, *Konstitutsionno-Pravovye Aspekty Protivodeistviia Ekstremizmu* [*Constitutional Aspects of Counteraction to Extremism*], ROSSIISKAIA IUSTITSIIA No. 3, 2011, at 62 (in Russian).

[4] Article 19's Statement on Proposed Amendments to the Russian Extremism Law at 1 (July 2006), http://www.article19.org/data/files/pdfs/press/russia-extremism-law.pdf, *archived at* https://perma.cc/252S-8PUM.

[5] Anatolii Pchelintsev, *Zakonodatel'naia Praktika I Problemy Razgranicheniia Predmetov Vedeniia Rossiiskoi Federatsii I ee Sub'ektov v Sfere Svobody Sovesti I Veroispovedaniia* [*Legislative Practice and Problems of Delimitation of Jurisdiction of the Russian Federation and its Subjects in the Area of Freedom of Conscience and Religion*], ROSSIISKAIA IUSTITSIIA No. 1, 2011, at 63 (in Russian).

[6] Vladimir Kashepov, *Osobennosti Kvalifikatsii Prestuplenii Ekstremistskoi Napravlennosti* [*Particulars of Qualification of Extremist Crimes*], KOMMENTARII SUDEBNOI PRAKTIKI No. 13, 2007, at 94 (in Russian).

[7] *Mizulina Proposes Adding Orthodoxy to the Constitution* (in Russian), LENTA.RU (Nov. 22, 2013), http://lenta.ru/news/2013/11/22/constitution (translation by author), *archived at* http://perma.cc/YM62-QDLB.

[8] Federal'nyi Zakon RF o Protivodeistvii Ekstremistskoi Deiatel'nosti [Federal Law of the Russian Federation on Countering Extremist Activity (Extremism Law)], ROSSIISKAIA GAZETA [ROS. GAZ.], July 25, 2002.

[9] UGOLOVNYI KODEKS ROSSIISKOI FEDERATSII [UK RF] [CRIMINAL CODE], ROS. GAZ., June 13, 18, 19, 20, 25, 1996.

Code of Administrative Violations of the Russian Federation (Administrative Code),[10] and relevant norms included in more than twenty other laws regulating public associations, religious activities, public gatherings, mass media publications, the investigative work of law enforcement authorities, and other matters.[11]

The determining factor in qualifying an activity as extremist is the suspect's motivation.[12] Crimes motivated by prejudice or, as stated in Russian law, "ideological, political, racial, national or religious enmity, as well as hatred or enmity towards a social group," are classified as extremist crimes under the Criminal Code.[13] An additional list of activities deemed to be extremist is stipulated by the Extremism Law. This list does not coincide with the list of extremist crimes defined by the Criminal Code.[14] Extremist activities as they are listed in the Extremism Law are subject to prosecution regardless of their consequences and the level of public danger. This allows for the application of restrictive measures to relatively insignificant offenses.[15]

"Terrorism" is distinguished from "extremism" in that the former generally involves violent acts and pursues specific goals of exercising influence on governmental decision making by violating public security or frightening the population. Russian scholars believe that the distinctive feature of terrorism is the purpose of the crime, whereas extremist crimes are distinguished by the offender's motivation.[16] The continuing and diverse nature of extremist activities is also contrasted with the transitory nature of terrorist acts.[17] However, it appears that the Extremism Law treats terrorism as one of several extremist activities regardless of whether it was motivated by ideological, political, racial, national, or religious hatred.[18]

According to official statements, the necessity to fight terrorism was the main reason for developing anti-extremist legislation. However, Russian legal observers state that it cannot meet this purpose and that the expansion of acts that can be considered extremist crimes, and the doubling of the number of materials recognized as extremist and included in the list of banned publications in 2011, led to a situation where "anything from a criminal fiction to a

---

[10] KODEKS ROSSIISKOI FEDERATSII OB ADMINISTRATIVNYKH PRAVONARUSHENIAKH [KOAP RF] [CODE OF ADMINISTRATIVE VIOLATIONS], ROS. GAZ., Dec. 31, 2001.

[11] Sigarev, *supra* note 3, at 62.

[12] RASHID SABITOV ET AL., PRAVOVYE MERY PROTIVODEISTVIIA EKSTREMISTKSOI PRESTUPNOSTI: MONOGRAFIIA [LEGAL MEASURES COUNTERACTING EXTREMIST CRIME: MONOGRAPH] 8 (Chelyabinsk, 2009) (in Russian).

[13] UK RF art. 282.1.

[14] OLGA KORSHUNOVA, PRESTUPLENIIA EKSTREMISTSKOGO KHARAKTERA, TEORIIA I PRAKTIKA PROTIVODEISTVIIA [CRIMES OF EXTREMIST NATURE, THEORY AND PRACTICE OF COUNTERACTION] 153 (Saint Petersburg, 2006) (in Russian).

[15] SOVA CENTER FOR INFORMATION AND ANALYSIS (SOVA CENTER), THE STRUCTURE OF RUSSIAN ANTI-EXTREMIST LEGISLATION 1 (Nov. 2010), *available at* http://www.europarl.europa.eu/mcctdocs/2009_2014/documents/_droi/dv/201/201011/_20101129_3_10sova_en.pdf, *archived at* http://perma.cc/242Q-68EY.

[16] SABITOV ET AL., *supra* note 12, at 43.

[17] Kashepov, *supra* note 6, at 187.

[18] SABITOV ET AL., *supra* note 12, at 10.

postmodernist painting can be viewed as extremist."[19]   Because of the nature of the legislation and problems with its enforcement, "public trust in anti-extremist legislation and the government's ability to fight extremism through the existing legal arsenal was lost completely."[20]

In its report on the illegal application of anti-extremist legislation in Russia in 2012, the SOVA Center stated that while religious organizations constituted the majority of those previously accused of committing crimes under the Extremism Law, social activists and opposition politicians have become a recent target of law enforcement authorities who use the Extremism Law to punish these people.[21]   Among the examples of recently initiated investigations and accusations of committing extremist crimes are cases where local journalists were prosecuted for publishing articles discussing neutral subjects such as the status of languages of varied Russian ethnic minorities and the dominant role of the Russian language in ethnic autonomous republics constituting the Russian Federation. Most of the time, these cases were used by local authorities to silence social activists and members of the opposition.[22]   Some Russian legal experts also believe that these cases are initiated by provincial law enforcement authorities to demonstrate their vigilance in fighting extremism because no other forms of extremism can be found.[23]

III. Analysis of Federal Law on Countering Extremist Activity

A. Definition of "Extremism"

The Extremism Law is a framework document that gives a definition of extremism, sets forth the fundamentals of the national policy in that area, and emphasizes the importance of preventive measures.[24]

Sanctions for extremist activity can be applied against organizations, mass media outlets, and individuals.[25]   It appears that organizations and mass media are the main targets of the Extremism Law.[26]   Organizations or media institutions may be punished under the Extremism Law for extremism *per se*. Individuals are punishable only in cases where their actions fall

---

[19] *282-e Preduprezhdenie [Warning No. 282]*, GAZETA.RU (Oct. 27, 2011), www.gazeta.ru/comments/2011/10/27 e_3814530.shtml (in Russian), *archived at* http://perma.cc/55JM-8759.

[20] *Id.* (translation by the authors).

[21] Maria Kravchenko, *Illegal Application of Anti-Extremist Legislation in Russia in 2012*, SOVA CENTER (Apr. 24, 2013), http://www.sova-center ru/misuse/publications/2013/04/d26952 (in Russian), *archived at* http://perma.cc/ ESK4-A7TR.

[22] Zhanna Ulianova, *In "Vziatka" Extremism Was Not Found Immediately*, GAZETA.RU (Aug. 22, 2012), http://www.gazeta.ru/social/2012/08/22/4733817.shtml (in Russian), *archived at* http://perma.cc/G36Y-S8BU.

[23] *Prosecution Found Extremism in a Three-Year-Old Article on Mordva Language*, NEWSRU.COM (Aug. 21, 2012), http://www.newsru.com/russia/21aug2012/inza_print.html (in Russian), *archived at* http://perma.cc/A24G-KZYQ.

[24] Kashepov, *supra* note 6, at 61.

[25] MOSCOW HELSINKI GROUP, NATIONALISM, XENOPHOBIA AND INTOLERANCE IN CONTEMPORARY RUSSIA 126 (2002), http://www.mhg.ru/english/1F65E50, *archived at* http://perma.cc/7NSU-H8GS.

[26] SOVA CENTER, *supra* note 15, at 1.

within the definition of an offense of extremism provided by the Criminal Code or the Code of Administrative Violations.[27]

The Extremism Law contains no clear definition of extremism. Instead there is an "extremely heterogeneous"[28] list of violent and nonviolent activities considered to be extremist, which includes

> forcible change of the foundations of the constitutional system and violation of integrity of the Russian Federation;

> public justification of terrorism and other terrorist activity;

> incitement of social, racial, ethnic or religious hatred;

> propaganda of exclusiveness, superiority or inferiority of an individual based on his/her social, racial, ethnic, religious or linguistic identity, or his/her attitude to religion;

> violation of rights, liberties and legitimate interests of an individual because of his/her social, racial, ethnic, religious or linguistic identity or attitude to religion;

> preventing citizens from exercising their electoral rights and the right to participate in a referendum, or violating the secrecy of the vote, combined with violence or threats to use violence;

> preventing legitimate activities of government authorities, local self-government, election commissions, public and religious associations or other organizations, combined with violence or threats to use violence;

> committing crimes involving the aggravating factors listed in article 63(1) of the Criminal Code (e.g., repeated crimes, crimes committed by an organized group, or crimes with severe consequences);

> propaganda and public demonstration of Nazi attributes or symbols, or attributes and symbols similar to them or public demonstration of attributes or symbols of extremist organizations;

> mass distribution of materials known to be extremist, their production and possession for the purposes of distribution;

> dissemination of knowingly false accusations against federal or regional officials in their official capacity, alleging that they have committed illegal or criminal acts; [and]

> organization and preparation of extremist acts, and calls to commit them; and
> financing the above-mentioned acts or providing any other material support to an extremist organization, including assistance in printing their materials, offering

---

[27] *Id.* at 1.

[28] *Id.*

educational or technical facilities, or providing communications or information services.[29]

This list has been criticized for duplicating provisions of the Criminal Code[30] and for failing to indicate objectives distinguishing extremist activities from other offenses.[31] The definition of extremism became even broader after 2006 amendments, which extended the definition of extremism and allowed for the prosecution of those who criticize federal and local governments and officials, official policies, laws, ideas, religious and political organizations, etc.[32] In June 2011, the Supreme Court, ruling on the application of the Extremism Law in courts, added to this ambiguity by stating that criticizing the professional activities of politicians and government officials must not always be considered as an incitement of hatred and enmity, and must be reviewed by courts on a case-by-case basis, because limits for criticizing such persons are broader than for private individuals.[33] (For a discussion of the constitutionality of these amendments see Part VI of this report.) The lack of certainty was noted by the Russian Ombudsman, who stated in his 2008 report that no one publicly criticizing the state, its policy, and public officials, even with a good understanding of the current legislation, can predict whether his words contain signs of extremism.[34] Even Russia's Foreign Ministry allegedly admitted that the definition of extremism in Russia is "too broad."[35] Human rights organizations have reportedly suggested that some clarifications preventing such a broad application of the Extremism Law should be added because explanatory guidelines issued by the Russian Federation Supreme Court in 2011[36] do not prevent abuses in the application of this Law.[37] As an example of such clarifications, scholars cite article 16 of the Russian Federal Law on Public Associations, which states that the inclusion of provisions on the protection of ideals of social

---

[29] Extremism Law art. 1(1) (translation by authors).

[30] Olga Mukhina, *Politiko-Pravovye Tekhnologii Bor'by s Ekstremizmom v Rossii (Opyt Primeneniia Federal'nogo Zakona RF ot 25 iiulia 2002 goda "O Protivodeistvii Eekstremistskoi Deiatel'nosti")* [*Political and Legal Technologies to Combat Extremism in Russia (Experience of Applying Federal Law of the Russian Federation of 25 July 2002 on Counteracting Extremist Activity)*], 2(7) ROSSIISKIAIA AKADEMIIA IURIDICHESKIKH NAUK, NAUCHNYE TRUDY 484 (2007) (in Russian).

[31] Igor Petin, *Sistemnyi Podkhod k Obespecheniiu Effektivnosti Preduprejdeniia Ekstremizma* [*Systematic Approach to Ensuring Effectiveness of Extremism Prevention*], ROSSIISKII SLEDOVATEL' No. 18, 2009, at 23 (in Russian).

[32] Sigarev, *supra* note 3, at 62.

[33] Ruling of the Supreme Court of the Russian Federation No. 11 of June 28, 2011, on Resolving Extremism-Related Criminal Cases by Courts § 7, ROS. GAZ. No. 5518, July 4, 2011.

[34] DOKLAD UPOLNOMOCHENNOGO PO PRAVAM CHELOVEKA V ROSSIISKOI FEDERATSII ZA 2008 GOD [REPORT OF THE COMMISSIONER FOR HUMAN RIGHTS IN THE RUSSIAN FEDERATION IN 2008] (Feb. 17, 2009), http://www.rg.ru/2009/04/17/doklad-lukin-dok.html (in Russian), *cited in* Sigarev, *supra* note 3, at 63, *archived at* http://perma.cc/CDB4-A5ZJ.

[35] *Predstavitel' Tsentra "SOVA" vystupil na slushaniiakh v Evroparlamente* [*The Representative of the SOVA Center Spoke at the Hearing in the European Parliament*], SOVA CENTER (Dec. 1, 2010), http://www.sova-center.ru/misuse/publications/2010/12/d20411 (in Russian), *archived at* http://perma.cc/J5GE-6R76.

[36] Ruling of the Supreme Court, *supra* note 33.

[37] GAZETA.RU, *supra* note 19.

justice in the constituent and policy documents of public associations may not be regarded as inciting social enmity.[38]

Some Russian experts believe that the definition of extremism was interpreted too broadly by the Supreme Court in 2012,[39] when the Court upheld the decision of a lower court finding elements of a crime under article 280 of the Russian Criminal Code (public calls for performance of an extremist activity) for an individual's participation in a political organization that had the declared goal of "chang[ing] the Putin-Medvedev regime, eliminat[ing] monopoly in politics and information, democratization of the country, and the refusal to cooperate with current power authorities."[40]

B. Enforcement of the Extremism Law

The main sanction provided by the Extremism Law is the liquidation of a public association, organization, or mass media outlet, which may be preceded by one or more warnings issued by the Federal Registration Service against a nongovernment organization or the Federal Supervision Agency for Information Technologies and Communications (Roskomnadzor) against media institutions. Local prosecutor's offices can issue warnings to both public and media organizations.[41] In 2010, the Federal Security Service was granted the power to issue warnings to individuals regarding the unacceptability of actions that may be seen as leading to the commission of crimes prosecuted under article 280 of the Criminal Code.[42] The procedural status of such warnings is not clear because they are not mentioned in the Criminal Procedural Code of the Russian Federation.

If the acts cited in the warning are not corrected or if something similar to what prompted the initial warning happens again, a prosecutor or registering authority may file a liquidation suit with the court in the place where the organization is registered. Liquidation charges can be brought against an organization even without warning if the organization's activities resulted or could have resulted in some unspecified damage.[43] In the latter case, the prosecutor or a local department of the Ministry of Justice may decide to suspend the operations of the organization while the liquidation suit is pending.[44] A decision to suspend the operation of a media outlet can

---

[38] Federal'nyi Zakon RF ob Obsh'estvennykh Ob'edineniakh [Federal Law of the Russian Federation on Public Associations], ROS. GAZ., May 25, 1995.

[39] *Full Right to Eavesdrop*, EKSPERT (Dec. 17, 2012), http://expert.ru/expert/2012/50/slushaem--i-imeem-polnoe-pravo/ (in Russian), *archived at* http://perma.cc/D3KM-JMKU.

[40] Ruling of the Russian Federation Supreme Court No. 45-U12-1079 of November 12, 2012, case information *at* http://supcourt.ru/vs_cases3.php?card=1&name_comp=%CF%E5%F2%EB%E8%ED&number_comp=&search.x=3 1&search.y=6, *archived at* http://perma.cc/TEM3-5RD3, full text available in Russian *at* http://www.yabloko.ru/files/petlin.pdf, *archived at* http://perma.cc/33HT-UGRZ.

[41] SOVA CENTER, *supra* note 15, at 3.

[42] Maria Rozalskaya, *Inappropriate Enforcement of Anti-extremist Legislation in Russia in 2010*, SOVA CENTER (Apr. 11, 2011), http://www.sova-center.ru/en/misuse/reports-analyses/2011/04/d21360/, *archived at* http://perma.cc/3AR6-PDYC.

[43] MOSCOW HELSINKI GROUP, *supra* note 25, at 127.

[44] *Id.*

be made by the court only upon request from a prosecutor or registering authorities.[45] A nonregistered organization may simply be banned for extremist activities. Participation in an extremist organization that has been liquidated or banned constitutes a separate crime.[46]

On July 15, 2010, the Supreme Court ruled that media outlets cannot be held responsible for xenophobic statements if they publish satirical, humorous, and unrealistic materials on "extremist" topics, and for audience comments during live broadcasts or on Internet forums. The Supreme Court also instructed the lower courts to consider the entire content and context of the publication.[47] However, after the Supreme Court's decision a lower court upheld a warning issued against a newspaper for a cartoon depicting a swastika.[48] This decision was based on a previously issued Supreme Court ruling that the publication of propaganda depicting swastikas and Nazi symbols constitutes a sufficient ground for banning the organization using such symbols.[49]

C. Lists of Banned Materials and Organizations

The Extremism Law imposes on the Ministry of Justice an obligation to complete, update, and publish a list of extremist materials. Maintaining such a list allows enforcement agencies to take administrative measures to restrict the distribution of extremist materials included in the list under article 20.29 of the Code of Administrative Violations, which prohibits the production and distribution of extremist materials. This provision is reportedly used against producers and distributors of materials included in the list in cases where instituting criminal proceedings under articles 280 and 282 of the Criminal Code would be inappropriate or complicated[50] due to the fact that prosecutors are required to prove intent to incite hatred and enmity in order to institute criminal charges.[51]

Currently, the Federal List of Extremist Materials includes 2,280 items.[52] It is not clear whether inclusion of a title in the list means that only the material with certain output data—for example,

---

[45] Federal'nyi Zakon RF o Sredstvakh Massovoi Informatsii [Federal Law of the Russian Federation on Mass Media], ROS. GAZ., Feb. 8, 1992.

[46] SOVA CENTER, *supra* note 15, at 4.

[47] Rozalskaya, *supra* note 42.

[48] *Id.*

[49] Opredelenie Verkhovnogo Suda RF 18-G07-1 ot 6 fevralia 2007 g., p.3. [Part 3 of the Russian Federation Supreme Court Ruling 18-G07-1 of Feb. 6, 2007], BIULLETEN' VERKHOVNOGO SUDA RF [BVS] [Bulletin of the Supreme Court of the Russian Federation] 2007, No. 12 (in Russian).

[50] SOVA CENTER, XENOPHOBIA, FREEDOM OF CONSCIENCE AND ANTI-EXTREMISM IN RUSSIA IN 2009: A COLLECTION OF ANNUAL REPORTS BY THE SOVA CENTER FOR INFORMATION AND ANALYSIS 82 (Moscow, Apr. 2010), http://www.sova-center.ru/files/books/pe10-text.pdf, *archived at* http://perma.cc/CS5M-VBVQ.

[51] Ruling of the Supreme Court, *supra* note 33.

[52] *Federal'nyi Spisok Ekstremistskikh Materialov* [*Federal List of Extremist Materials*], MINISTRY OF JUSTICE, *available at* http://minjust.ru/extremist-materials (in Russian; last visited Apr. 7, 2014), *archived at* http://perma.cc/6DLT-W4KR.

a particular edition of a book—is banned or whether the ban applies to all forms of the publication, including its textual and audiovisual variations.[53]
Also, the list includes several dozen files that cannot be identified[54] because they are locally distributed leaflets dedicated to current events, websites that no longer exist, or private posts on Internet forums.[55] If a forum statement is considered extremist by Roskomnadzor, a formal letter is emailed and faxed to the editor, and an official warning is issued unless the commentary is removed within twenty-four hours.[56]

Materials added to the list are usually categorized as the following: racist, xenophobic and anti-Semitic materials; materials of Jehovah's Witnesses; materials of North Caucasus separatists and other radical Islamists; materials of the Church of Scientology; and materials of different Muslim groups, generally not related to officially recognized Islamic organizations.[57] In addition, thirty-four organizations appear on the list as banned or liquidated for extremist activities.[58] Most of the banned organizations are Russian patriotic and religious organizations propagating racist and xenophobic ideas, seven Muslim groups, and one religious community of Jehovah's Witnesses.

According to the SOVA Center for Information and Analysis, while at least three earlier bans were removed in 2009, there is no established mechanism for delisting materials.[59] Reportedly, information placed on the list does not meet bibliographical standards and researchers have no access to banned materials. Also, it is not clear if the ban officially begins when the decision of the court enters into force or when the material is listed.[60] On March 4, 2014, two brochures published by Jehovah's Witnesses and recognized by a Russian regional court as nonextremist in February of 2012 were removed from the list of banned materials.[61]

---

[53] Vera Alperovich & Galina Kozhevnikova, *Autumn 2010: The Ultra-right in Search of a New Strategy*, SOVA CENTER (Jan. 14, 2011), http://www.sova-center.ru/en/misuse/reports-analyses/2011/01/d20707, *archived at* http://perma.cc/YU3S-E2V7.

[54] Aleksandr Verkhovskii & Galina Kozhevnikova, *Prizrak Manejnoi Plosh'adi: Radikal'nyi Natsionalizm v Rossii i Protivodeistvie Emu v 2010 godu* [*Phantom of Manege Square: Radical Nationalism and the Counteraction to It in 2010*], SOVA CENTER (Mar. 11, 2011), http://www.sova-center.ru/racism-xenophobia/publications/2011/03/d21140/ (in Russian), *archived at* http://perma.cc/TR8W-N4U6.

[55] SOVA CENTER, *supra* note 50, at 42.

[56] Maria Rozalskaya, *supra* note 42.

[57] Aleksandr Verkhovskii & Galina Kozhevnikova, *supra* note 54.

[58] *Perechen'Oobschesvennykh I Religioznykh Ob'edenenii, Inykh Nekommercheskikh Organizatsii, v Otnoshenii Kotorykh Sudom Priniato Vstupivshee v Zakonnuiu Silu Reshenie o Likvidatsii ili Zaprete Deiatel'nosti po Osnovaniiam, Predusmotrennym Federal'nym Zakonom "O Protivodeistvii Ekstremistskoi Deiatel'nosti"* [*List of Public Organizations and Other Nonprofit Organizations with Regard to which the Court has Adopted a Decision Entered into Force to Liquidate or Ban the Activities on the Grounds Provided by the Federal Law on Counteraction to Extremist Activity*], MINISTERSTVO JUSTITSII [MINISTRY OF JUSTICE], http://www.minjust.ru/nko/perechen_zapret (in Russian) (last visited Apr. 7, 2014), *archived at* http://perma.cc/ZPV2-Q4XP.

[59] SOVA CENTER, *supra* note 50, at 42.

[60] *Id.* at 43.

[61] *Jehovah's Witnesses' Brochures Removed from the Federal List of Extremist Materials*, SOVA CENTER (Mar. 4, 2014), http://www.sova-center.ru/misuse/news/counteraction/2014/03/d29084/ (in Russian), *archived at* http://perma.cc/6V57-CZ9W.

D. Non-Criminal Liability of Individuals Prosecuted for Extremism

In addition to criminal or administrative punishment for extremist activities, which may take the form of a limitation of freedom, imprisonment, correctional labor, or a fine, the rights of people prosecuted for extremist activities may also be restricted in other ways. An individual convicted for extremist activity might be limited in his access to public service or contractual military service, may not be employed by law enforcement agencies and educational institutions, and may not engage in private detective and security activities.[62]

Organizations can be held responsible for the extremist activities of their leaders. If leaders of an organization are found to be engaged in extremist activities, the organization must officially disassociate itself from their actions.[63] Otherwise, the organization is subject to the repressive measures specified in the Extremism Law, whereas the leaders are prosecuted under the Criminal Code.[64] Organizations and individuals involved in extremist activities are included in the blacklist published by the federal agency for financial monitoring and are subject to having their accounts and transactions frozen.[65] Following the amendments to the Law on Freedom of Conscience and Religious Associations passed in July 2013, a ban on establishing religious organizations or becoming a member of such an organization was extended to individuals in whose actions Russian courts found signs of extremist activity.[66]

If a political candidate conducts extremist activities during an election campaign, he may be banned by a court decision from participating in elections. Such a ban may result from prior statements made during a period equal to his potential term in office if such statements included calls for extremist activity, justification of such activity, or incitement of hatred.[67]

Foreign citizens responsible for extremist conduct can be denied entry into Russia, as was the case for a German couple leading a local branch of Jehovah's Witnesses.[68]

---

[62] Extremism Law art. 15, para. 2, *as amended by* Federal Law No. 185-FZ of July 2, 2013, ROS. GAZ. No. 148, July 10, 2013.

[63] SOVA CENTER, *supra* note 15, at 3.

[64] ROS. GAZ., *supra* note 8, art. 15.

[65] Sergei Smirnov & Anna Cherkasova, *DPNI i NBP v Spiske s Terrosistami* [*MAII and NBP on the Terrorist List*], GAZETA.RU (July 6, 2011), http://www.gazeta.ru/politics/2011/07/06_a_3687413.shtml, *archived at* http://perma.cc/F7KM-CC9P.

[66] Federal Law of July 2, 2013 No. 180-FZ On Amendments to Article 9 of the Federal Law On Freedom of Conscience and Religious Associations, ROS. GAZ. No. 145, Jul. 5, 2013.

[67] SOVA CENTER, *supra* note 15, at 5.

[68] VLADIMIR KASHEPOV ET AL., PRAVOVOE PROTIVODEISTVIE EKSTREMIZMU [LEGAL COUNTERACTION TO EXTREMISM] 41 (Moscow, 2008) (in Russian).

IV. Prosecution of Extremist Crimes and Misdemeanors Under the Criminal and Administrative Codes

A. Criminal Code Provisions

Article 282 of the Russian Criminal Code defines extremist crimes as those motivated by ideological, political, racial, national, or religious enmity, as well as hatred or enmity towards a social group. Extremist motivation can be a required or alternative element of a crime, and may warrant a more severe punishment, similar to crimes committed with aggravating circumstances.[69]

Extremist motivation is a required element of the following crimes: inciting hatred or enmity, or demeaning human dignity (art. 282); organizing an extremist community (art. 282.1-bis); organizing the activity of an extremist community (art. 282.2-bis); and genocide (art. 357). Extremism-related crimes are punishable with varied fines, corrective labor, different forms of deprivation of freedom, and imprisonment for up to six years for the most serious extremist acts, which involve forming and participating in an organized extremist community.

An "extremist community" within the meaning of article 282.1-bis is a settled group of people associated in advance to prepare and commit one or more crimes of an extremist nature, characterized by the presence of a leader, stability of composition, and coherence of the actions of its members aimed at achieving a common criminal purpose.[70]

Article 282.2-bis treats as a criminal offense the leadership of or participation in an extremist organization, i.e., one that has been liquidated or banned by a court.[71] This article was used to impose sentences on members of the National Bolshevik Party and Hizb ut-Tahrir solely for attending events organized by these organizations.[72]

In February 2014, the Criminal Code of the Russian Federation was amended to add provisions aimed at increasing punishments for extremism-related crimes.[73] The new provisions doubled the duration of mandatory correctional labor and nearly tripled the amount of fines for extremist crimes, making the maximum fine equal to approximately US$17,000. As stated in explanatory documents to this Law submitted to the legislature by the President's Administration, these amendments were needed to "neutralize threats to national security caused by destructive activities of religious organizations on the Russian territory."[74]

---

[69] SABITOV ET AL., *supra* note 12, at 101; VIACHESLAV LEBEDEV, COMMENTARIES TO THE CRIMINAL CODE 710 (Moscow: Iurait, 2010).

[70] SOVA CENTER, *supra* note 50 at 87.

[71] MOSCOW HELSINKI GROUP, *supra* note 25, at 128.

[72] SOVA CENTER, *supra* note 50, at 89.

[73] Federal Law No. 5-FZ, on Amendments to the Criminal Code and Article 31 of the Criminal Procedural Code of the Russian Federation, ROS. GAZ. No. 6296, Feb. 5, 2014.

[74] *Putin Created Military Police and Harshened Punishments for Extremism*, NEWSRU.COM (Feb. 4, 2014), http://www.newsru.com/russia/04feb2014/voenpolic.html (in Russian), *archived at* http://perma.cc/FX8A-8XYH.

Additionally, the law changed the venue where extremism-related cases are tried. Because crimes containing the elements of extremism were reclassified as crimes of medium gravity, these cases were removed from the jurisdiction of justices of the peace and were included in the jurisdiction of federal district courts.[75]

Extremism is an alternative motivation and an aggravating circumstance for the following crimes: violation of the equality of human and civil rights and freedoms (art. 136), hooliganism (art. 213), and public appeals for the performance of an extremist activity (art. 280).[76] Other scholars add to this list terrorism (art. 205), hostage-taking (art. 206), destruction or damage to historic or cultural monuments (art. 243), outrages upon the bodies of the deceased and their burial places (art. 244), threatening the life of a statesman or a public figure (art. 247), forcible seizure of power or forcible retention of power (art. 248), armed rebellion (art. 249), and mercenary activities (art. 359).[77] Because extremist motivation is specifically listed among aggravating circumstances for a number of crimes, it must be taken into account for purposes of sentencing (art. 63). The advocacy organization Human Rights First has reported, however, that enhanced penalties under article 63 are not regularly sought or applied.[78] In addition to the general rule stated in article 63, a number of the Code's provisions specifically provide for more severe punishment when prejudice is shown in particular crimes, e.g., murder (art. 105), deliberate infliction of injuries or bodily harm (arts. 111, 112), torture (art. 117), and desecration of cemeteries (art. 244).

According to the SOVA Center, virtually all relevant provision of the Criminal Code are used in prosecuting perpetrators of violent crimes,[79] although there has been a general perception that charges of hooliganism are routinely pressed by prosecution authorities even when more serious crimes are committed.[80] According to the reports of Russian human rights defenders, this is often due to the inability of law enforcement authorities to properly examine and evaluate the motivation behind a crime.[81] Reportedly, in order to hide their obvious reasons for committing a hate crime, ultra-right Russian organizations distribute "instructions" to their members, in which they recommend committing robberies as a means of disguising the real hate motivation of a crime.[82]

In June 2013, a few month after three members of the Russian feminist group known as Pussy Riot were sentenced to two years' imprisonment for "hooliganism motivated by religious hatred"

---

[75] Federal Law No. 5-FZ.

[76] SABITOV ET AL., *supra* note 12, at 101.

[77] KASHEPOV ET AL., *supra* note 68, at 30.

[78] PAUL LEGENDRE, HUMAN RIGHTS FIRST, MINORITIES UNDER SIEGE: HATE CRIMES AND INTOLERANCE IN THE RUSSIAN FEDERATION 4 (June 26, 2006), http://www.humanrightsfirst.org/wp-content/uploads/ pdf/06623-discrim-Minorities-Under-Siege-Russia-web.pdf, *archived at* http://perma.cc/4ZWH-HFTN.

[79] SOVA CENTER, *supra* note 50, at 6.

[80] MOSCOW HELSINKI GROUP, *supra* note 25, at 5.

[81] KORSHUNOVA, *supra* note 14, at 169.

[82] SOVA CENTER, *supra* note 50, at 38.

after performing inside a Russian Orthodox church in Moscow, the State Duma adopted amendments to the Criminal Code on "protecting . . . religious feelings of believers." [83] The provisions amended article 148 of the Criminal Code by establishing penalties, such as fines, corrective works, and deprivation of freedom for up to two years, for the public insult of religious convictions and feelings of citizens and of religious ceremonies. [84]

The SOVA Center has noted that the authorities rarely impose sentences involving prison time for nonviolent racist propaganda. [85] Other sanctions, in addition to suspended sentences, are typically imposed for minor acts, such as painting graffiti, distribution of flyers, or writing posts on Web forums and blogs. [86] Suspended sentences are also used in situations where cases are initiated against government opponents or followers of public or religious organizations not supported by the authorities. On November 3, 2011, a provincial court sentenced a local Jehovah's Witness activist to one hundred hours of community service after the local administration insisted on punishing him even though the court had initially acquitted him. [87] It appears that the number of suspended sentences without additional sanctions has constantly increased and constituted 43% of all sentences pronounced in 2010. [88] According to available statistics, in 2010 there was only one hate crimes case in which a perpetrator received prison time; the case involved one of the most infamous anti-Semitic journalists, who was sentenced to a three-year term served at a colony-settlement with a ban on editorial and journalistic activities. [89]

Russian law enforcement agencies have been targeting religious groups outside the Orthodox community for "extremism." For example, multiple cases have been opened and several court decisions issued with respect to the publication and distribution of religious texts by Jehovah's Witnesses and Muslims, including Muslim texts with quotations from the Koran.

Such literature was considered extremist and was subject to a ban on distribution throughout Russia. It was included on the Federal List of Extremist Materials, and individuals involved in its publication and distribution were found guilty of committing extremism-related criminal and

---

[83] *Russia at the UPR: Repeal Oppressive Laws Restricting the Rights to Freedom of Expression, Assembly and Association*, ARTICLE 19 (Apr.11, 2013), *at*: http://www.article19.org/resources.php/resource/3691/en/russia-at-the-upr:-repeal-oppressive-laws-restricting-the-rights-to-freedom-of-expression,-assembly-and-association#sthash. ZWdN6ubi.dpuf, *archived at* https://perma.cc/N5W4-35LS.

[84] Federal Law of the Russian Federation No. 136-FZ On Amendments to Article 148 of the Criminal Code of the Russian Federation and Certain Legislative Acts of the Russian Federation to Counter Insult of Religious Beliefs and Feelings of the Citizens, ROS. GAZ., No. 6117, Jul. 2, 2013.

[85] SOVA CENTER, *supra* note 50, at 6, 36.

[86] *Id.* at 37.

[87] Sophia Kishkovsky, *Russian Terror Law Has Unlikely Targets*, THE NEW YORK TIMES (Nov. 4, 2011), http://www.nytimes.com/2011/11/04/world/europe/russian-terror-law-has-unlikely-targets.html?_r=2&page wanted=print, *archived at* http://perma.cc/67JY-AJCT.

[88] Verkhovskii & Kozhevnikova, *supra* note 54.

[89] *Id.*

administrative offenses, usually under article 282 of the Criminal Code and article 20.29 of the Code of Administrative Violations.[90]

Authorities have been criticized for focusing too much on minor crimes and acts (e.g., prosecuting Internet trolls and graffiti artists),[91] and for prosecuting libraries and schools that were unable to follow updates to the Federal List of Extremist Materials and were found to be holding the banned books.[92]

B. Administrative Code Provisions

The following administrative offenses are or can be motivated by extremism: intentional public desecration of religious or theological literature, objects of religious veneration, signs or emblems, ideological symbols, and paraphernalia (art. 5.26, part 2); abusing freedom of mass information (art. 13.15); displaying fascist attributes and symbols (art. 20.3); organizing the activity of a social or religious organization against which a decision on suspension of activities was entered (art. 20.28); and producing and distributing extremist materials (art. 20.29).[93]

A new administrative liability provision was introduced in 2012 for the public display of extremist organizations' symbols. This type of activity is now considered a form of extremism and is punishable by a fine of up to approximately US$500 or detention for up to fifteen days. Fines for the display of Nazi symbols were similarly increased.[94] Article 20.3 of the Administrative Code is usually applied to impose penalties for selling Nazi paraphernalia and objects marked with swastikas, and for Nazi tattoos. In one such case, the court, in addition to imposing a fine on the defendant who had a Nazi tattoo, ordered him to have the tattoo removed.[95]

Article 20.29 is often interpreted broadly and is used to punish the distribution of works by the leaders of Nazi Germany as well as quoting those materials.[96] In 2010, a criminal prosecution was initiated in the city of Perm for placing stickers with Adolf Hitler's quote, "[w]e will defeat Russia when Ukrainians and Belarusians believe that they are not Russian," in city buses.[97]

---

[90] Geraldine Fagan, *Russia: Muslims Rush to Challenge Koran "Extremism" Ruling*, FORUM 18 (Sept. 27, 2013), http://www.forum18.org/archive.php?article_id=1879, *archived at* http://perma.cc/5SAW-B25A.

[91] SOVA CENTER, *supra* note 50, at 6.

[92] Alperovich & Kozhevnikova, *supra* note 53.

[93] Russian Federation Code of Administrative Violations, Federal Law No. 195-FZ, ROS. GAZ. No. 256, Dec. 31, 2001.

[94] Federal Law No. 255-FZ on Amendments to Selected Legal Acts art. 2, ROS. GAZ. No. 301, Dec. 28, 2012.

[95] SOVA CENTER, *supra* note 50, at 38.

[96] Alperovich & Kozhevnikova, *supra* note 53.

[97] Ilia Izotov, *V Permi Vozbuzhdeno Delo po Faktu Raskleiki Tsitat Gitlera v Tramvaiakh* [*Criminal Proceedings Have Been Initiated in Perm for Posting Hitler Quotations in the Tram*], ROS. GAZ., Oct. 8, 2010, http://www.rg.ru/2010/10/08/reg-permkray/stikeri-anons.html, *archived at* http://perma.cc/MMU7-M3DY (click "Uploaded page).

V. Procedural Aspects of Investigation

Experts play a central role in the investigation of hate crimes in Russia because the conclusion as to whether specific material or a statement made by a suspect appears to be extremist is based on an expert's opinion. The expert's participation is considered by all parties as an integral part of any extremist case,[98] except for cases involving items already included in the list of extremist materials.[99] The types of expert opinions sought by law enforcement bodies are sociopsychological and psycholinguistic (51%), relevant to political science (19%), philosophical (14%), linguistic (7%), sociological (4.5%), and ethnolinguistic (4.5%).[100] The law does not establish qualification requirements for experts, and they are usually chosen from among specialists of local scientific and educational institutions.[101] This practice will likely be restricted by a recent ruling of the Supreme Court, which prohibits experts from issuing opinions on legal issues, such as whether a text contains appeals to extremist activities and whether it aims to incite hatred or enmity.[102]

Presently, a person accused of committing a hate crime may choose to be tried by a jury or have his case heard by a professional judge or a panel of judges. Although the Ministry of Justice has recommended the removal of extremist crimes from the purview of jury trials to avoid nationalistic bias among jurors, it appears that guilty verdicts are issued evenly in bench and jury trials.[103] It appears that after a guilty verdict is delivered by the jury, judges issue minimal or suspended sentences.[104]

The investigation of extremist crimes is often delayed, and there are reports that prosecutors illegally refuse to initiate proceedings. The law enforcement officials explain this fact by pointing to the difficulty and length of investigations; the small number of independent experts knowledgeable in the fields of social psychology and psycholinguistics; the length of expert examinations, especially when materials are voluminous; and the lack of established investigative and judicial practices for this category of cases.[105] The majority of hate crime cases reported to the authorities by individuals or nongovernmental organizations, particularly those

---

[98] SOVA CENTER, *supra* note 50, at 79.

[99] Olga Dmitrenko, *Sud Samary Priznal Sait Dvizheniia "9 Maia" Ekstremistksim* [*Samara Court Declares the Website of "May 9" Movement Extremist*], ROS. GAZ., Oct. 13, 2010, *at* http://www.rg.ru/2010/10/13/reg-svolga/site-anons.html (in Russian), *archived at* http://perma.cc/VT92-KQSC (click "Uploaded page).

[100] VIKTORIA BURKOVSKAYA, KRIMINAL'NYI RELIGIOZNYI EKSTREMIZM V SOVREMENNOI ROSSII [CRIMINAL RELIGIOUS EXTREMISM IN MODERN RUSSIA] 145 (Moscow, 2005) (in Russian), *cited in* Andrei Pavlinov, *Kakie Nuzhny Ekspertizy dlia Protivodeistviia Sovremennomu Ekstremizmu v Rossii* [*What Expert Examinations Are Needed to Counteract Modern Extremism in Russia*], ROSSIISKII SLEDOVATEL' No. 2, 2008, at 6 (in Russian).

[101] Sigarev, *supra* note 3, at 62.

[102] *Kommentarii "SOVY" na Postanovlenie Plenuma Verkhovnogo Suda ob Ekstremizme* [*Commentary of "SOVA" on the Ruling of the Supreme Court on Extremism*], SOVA CENTER (July 2011), http://www.sova-center.ru/misuse/publications/2011/07/d22010/ (in Russian), *archived at* http://perma.cc/YC24-9S57.

[103] Rozalskaya, *supra* note 42.

[104] *Id.*

[105] KASHEPOV ET AL., *supra* note 68, at 162.

involving drawings of swastika images and extremist slogans, are suspended due to a failure to identify the responsible individuals.[106]

VI. Constitutional Issues Regarding the Prosecution of Extremism

Given the broad definition of "extremism," actions that do not fall within any category of crime or even an administrative offense can be qualified as extremist under the law and be subject to repressive measures.[107] The application of article 280 of the Criminal Code is especially vague. This provision is often used for prosecuting varied offenses when the government is demonstrating its interest in fighting extremism.[108] For example, criminal proceedings under article 280 were initiated against a seventy-one-year-old retiree who had expressed a willingness to carry out a death sentence against the governor of the region at a local protest against price increases.[109]

The term "social group" is subject to an especially broad interpretation for the purpose of applying article 282, which outlaws the incitement of hatred towards a social group,[110] because all groups, according to observers, are "social."[111] The introduction of this broad term can be explained by the legislator's concern that traditional groups based on race, nationality, and religion are too narrow and inadequate to protect other socially significant, numerous, and organized groups.[112]

Criticism of the distinctive features of a social group, if such criticism contributes to a negative image of that group as opposed to criticism of a particular individual or an idea, is viewed by linguistic experts as extremism.[113] In practice, anti-extremist legislation was applied to defend those who were not particularly vulnerable. Special protection was given to such social groups as "law enforcement personnel," "the military," "investigation service officials," "police officers," "state employees," "owners of Russian-made motor vehicles,"[114] "representatives of the government of the Tatarstan Republic,"[115] and "informal groups of young people."[116] For example, a Russian blogger was sentenced for making critical comments about police in his

---

[106] *Id.* at 164.

[107] MOSCOW HELSINKI GROUP, *supra* note 25, at 126.

[108] *Id.* at 128.

[109] KASHEPOV ET AL., *supra* note 68, at 73.

[110] UK RF art. 282.

[111] Mikhail Osadchii, *Sotsial'nyi Ekstremizm kak Ob'ekt Sudebno-Lingvisticheskoi Eskpertizy [Social Extremism as a Subject of Forensic Linguistic Examination]*, UGOLOVNYI PROTSESS No. 2, 2008, at 57 (in Russian).

[112] *Id.* at 57, 64.

[113] *Id.* at 60.

[114] SOVA CENTER, *supra* note 50, at 92.

[115] *Id.* at 91.

[116] Natalia Kuz'mina, *Ustanovlenie Motivov Pri Kvalifikatsii Prestuplenii Esktremistskoi Napravlennost: Problemy Praktiki Pravoprimeneniia [Determination of Motives in Qualifying Crimes of Extremist Nature: Problems of Law Enforcement Practice]*, ROSSIISKII SLEDOVATEL' No. 24, 2010, at 19 (in Russian).

blog.[117]   At the same time, a Russian court did not recognize homosexuals as a separate and definite social group within the meaning of article 282.[118]   Responding to concerns that treating government officials as a social group could lead to a complete ban on all criticism of the government in contradiction to the Constitution,[119] the Supreme Court, in a landmark ruling of June 28, 2011, held that public officials and professional politicians are not a social group as their interests should not be different from those of the state, and the level of acceptable criticism should be higher as compared to private persons.[120]   However, the Supreme Court did not clarify which social groups are covered by anti-extremist legislation.[121]

According to the same Supreme Court ruling, article 282 on incitement of hatred is applicable to statements justifying genocide, mass repression, deportations, and other illegal acts, including violence, against representatives of any ethnic, racial, religious, or other group.[122]   Extremist rhetoric can be prosecuted only if used publicly, whereas statements made at private gatherings are not covered by article 282.[123]   Criticism of political, ideological, and religious organizations and beliefs, and ethnic or religious customs, cannot by itself be treated as incitement of hatred or enmity.[124]

Despite the fact that freedom of speech, religion, and expression are declared by the Constitution, Russian jurisprudence does not have a developed concept of protected speech. It is a common practice to use article 282 of the Criminal Code against authors who criticize the Russian Orthodox Church or Russian national and religious policy,[125] or those who argue against the suggestion that modern Tatarstan and other territories "peacefully joined the Russian state."[126]   There have been instances of anti-extremist criminal prosecution of individuals who proposed referendums on separating several regions and annexing them to Finland, or who suggested constitutional amendments aimed at bringing public officials to justice.[127]

---

[117] *Blogger, Osuzhdennyi v RF za Prizyv "Szhigat' Mentov", Poluchil Politicheskoe Ubezhish'e v Estonii* [*The Blogger Convicted in the Russian Federation for Appeals to "Burn Cops" Was Granted Political Asylum in Estonia*], NEWSRU.COM, July 13, 2011, http://www.newsru.com/world/13jul2011/savva_print.html (in Russian), *archived at* http://perma.cc/7YHH-56CG.

[118] SOVA CENTER, *supra* note 50, at 93.

[119] *Id.* at 92.

[120] Ruling of the Supreme Court, *supra* note 33; *see also* SOVA CENTER, *supra* note 50; Peter Roudik, *Russian Federation: Government Takes Measures Against Extremism*, GLOBAL LEGAL MONITOR (Aug. 16, 2011), http://www.loc.gov/lawweb/servlet/lloc_news?disp3_l205402777_text, *archived at* http://perma.cc/9EH7-K24J.

[121] *Misuse of Anti-Extremism Legislation in June 2011*, SOVA CENTER (July 4, 2011), http://www.sova-center.ru/en/misuse/news-releases/2011/07/d22022, *archived at* http://perma.cc/FK3C-YDCJ.

[122] SOVA CENTER, *supra* note 50, at 85.

[123] Roudik, *supra* note 120.

[124] SOVA CENTER, *supra* note 50, at 85.

[125] *Id.* at 86.

[126] *Id.* at 87.

[127] Alperovich & Kozhevnikova, *supra* note 53.

Articles 282 (inciting hate) and 282.1-bis (establishing an extremist community), together with administrative penalties for distributing extremist materials, are often applied against Jehovah's Witnesses, the main religious group prosecuted on anti-extremist grounds.[128] Materials of the Church of Scientology have been banned because, according to experts, they contain appeals to extremist activity, as well as "humiliating characteristics, negative evaluation, and attitudes against persons on the basis of their social status."[129] Many undesirable religious groups have been prosecuted for propagating superiority based on religious identity, even though such propaganda appears to be common to many religious preachers.[130]

VII. Government Activities Aimed at Preventing Extremism

The Extremism Law notes the importance of preventive measures in articles 2 and 5 but does not describe such measures.[131]

The Interdepartmental Commission on Countering Extremism in the Russian Federation, an interagency governmental commission on counteracting extremist activities comprising the heads of sixteen government agencies, was created by order of the President on July 29, 2011.[132] The Commission is charged with proposing anti-extremist policies, developing relevant concepts and strategies, evaluating current activities, reviewing measures undertaken and legislation adopted, and preparing annual reports for the President.[133] The Commission held thirteen meetings through March 2013 (latest information available). The agendas of these meetings included discussions on improving legal regulations on countering extremist activities in Russia, such as toughening responsibility for unauthorized mass public actions and violations in the field of migration, prevention of terrorism and extremism, formation of Russian civic identity, and promotion of patriotism among Russia's youth. The Commission also encouraged the Russian Ministry of Internal Affairs (police) to create an interdepartmental working group on combating extremist ideology in the media and on the Internet.[134] A scientific advisory council for the study of religious materials aimed at detecting signs of extremism has been operating under the

---

[128] *Id.*

[129] Miriam Elder, *Russian Court Bans Scientology Books*, GLOBALPOST (June 30, 2011, 1:33 PM), http://www. globalpost.com/dispatches/globalpost-blogs/bric-yard/russian-court-bans-scientology-books, *archived at* http://perma.cc/HJP7-ENL2, *cited in* Galina Bryntseva, *"Prorok" ekstremistskogo roda. Rossiiskii sud zapretil raboty osnovatelia saientologii Rona Khabbarda* [*"Prophet" of Extremist Nature. Russian Court Bans the Works of the Founder of Scientology Ron Hubbard*], ROS. GAZ., July 4, 2011, http://www.rg.ru/2011/07/04/habbard.html (in Russian), *archived at* http://perma.cc/3UXW-8APA (click "Uploaded page").

[130] KASHEPOV ET AL., *supra* note 68, at 39.

[131] Sigarev, *supra* note 3, at 62.

[132] Ukaz Prezidenta RF o Mezhvedomstvennoi Komissii po Protivodeistviu Ekstremizmu v Rossiiskoi Federatsii [Decree of the President of the Russian Federation on Interdepartmental Commission to Counteract Extremism], SOBRANIE ZAKONODATEL'STVA RF [COLLECTION OF LEGISLATION OF THE RF] 2011, No. 988 Item 4705.

[133] *Id.*

[134] Activities of the Commission are conducted according to Statute on the Commission attached to the President's Decree 988 of July 26, 2011, http://pravo.gov.ru/proxy/ips/?docbody=&firstDoc=1&lastDoc=1&nd=102149658 (official publication, in Russian), *archived at* http://perma.cc/LJ5T-V4SJ.

Ministry of Justice since September 2009. The council issues advisory opinions on materials submitted by judicial and law enforcement bodies and private parties.[135]

VIII. International Cooperation in Fighting Extremism

Russia has signed a number of international documents providing for cooperation in fighting extremism and terrorism, particularly within the framework of regional organizations, such as the Shanghai Cooperation Organization (SCO), Commonwealth of Independent States, Eurasian Economic Community, and Collective Security Treaty Organization.[136] An example is the Concept of Cooperation Between SCO Member States in Combating Terrorism, Separatism, and Extremism, which provides for concerted preventive activities, operational search and investigative actions, the exchange of search and forensic information, the creation of specialized databases and communication systems, joint academic research, and cooperation in other areas.[137]

Russia is also a party to the Shanghai Convention on the Fight Against Terrorism, Separatism and Extremism of June 15, 2001, which emphasizes the violent nature of extremism in the definition provided in article 1(3). The Shanghai Convention's definition thus appears to be narrower than the Russian definition set forth in the Extremism Law, which covers both violent and nonviolent activities.[138]

---

[135] *Pri Miniuste Sozdan Sovet po Izucheniiu Religioznykh Materialov na Predmet Vyiavleniia v nikh Priznakow Ekstremizma* [*A Council for Examination of Religious Materials for Purposes of Detecting Signs of Extremism Has Been Created Under the Ministry of Justice*], SOVA CENTER (Sept. 23, 2009), http://www.sova-center.ru/religion/news/authorities/legal-regulation/2009/09/d16916/ (in Russian), *archived at* http://perma.cc/MDX5-KSVT.

[136] KASHEPOV ET AL., *supra* note 68, at 224.

[137] Concept of Cooperation Between SCO Member States in Combating Terrorism, Separatism, and Extremism Adopted by Resolution No. 1 of 5 June 2005 of the Council of Heads of SCO Member States, *available at* https://www.fidh.org/en/issues/terrorism/Concept-of-Cooperation-Between-SCO, *archived at* https://perma.cc/GB9E-YVYM.

[138] SABITOV ET AL., *supra* note 12, at 8 (citing Shanghai Convention on Combating Terrorism, Separation and Extremism, June 15, 2001, *available at* http://www.refworld.org/docid/49f5d9f92.html, *archived at* http://perma.cc/L5H3-26D7 (click "Uploaded page")).

Tajikistan

Peter Roudik
Director of Global Legal Research Directorate[*]

SUMMARY   The fight against extremism in Tajikistan is aimed at preventing extremism and punishing those who are involved in extremist activities. The necessity of fighting extremism is used by the government to justify its restrictions on religious freedom and its control over religious education and circulation of religious literature. Organizations and individuals can be held administratively and criminally liable for violating antiextremist legislation or committing other crimes if these crimes were motivated by hatred. Such offenders are most often accused of disseminating religious hatred.

I. Background Information

The long-lasting civil war in Tajikistan during the 1990s reflected the conflicts that had long existed in the society and, according to some scholars, motivated the engagement of the followers of radical Islamic ideology in the political life of the country.[1] Backed by support from radical groups in Pakistan and Afghanistan, these Islamists proposed their own path of reforms, which required building a society based on Islam, implementing Shari'a law, and opposing efforts of the ruling elite to build a secular country.[2] Even though the government has been successful in pursuing its policy of building a secular society, Tajikistan more than any other Central Asian state is considered susceptible to Islamic extremism, a fact that has shaped the reality of strict government control over freedom of religion.[3]

About 85% of Tajikistan's population consists of Sunni Muslims, while 5% follow Shi'a Islam and 10% profess other religions.[4] Islam is especially strong among the rural population.[5] It appears that the unemployed and those who have experienced dramatic changes in social status are the most active followers of Islam.[6]

---

[*] This report was last updated in May 2014. Foreign law consultants Virab Khachatryan and Svitlana Vodyanyk contributed to the report.

[1] ELENA BURKHANOVA ET AL., EKSTREMISM V CENTRAL'NOI AZII [EXTREMISM IN CENTRAL ASIA] 21 (Almaty, 2000) (in Russian).

[2] LENA JONSON, TAJIKISTAN IN THE NEW CENTRAL ASIA: GEOPOLITICS, GREAT POWER RIVALRY AND RADICAL ISLAM 96 (I.B. Tauris, 2006).

[3] BURKHANOVA ET AL., *supra* note 1.

[4] *Tajikistan, in* CENTRAL INTELLIGENCE AGENCY (CIA), THE WORLD FACTBOOK, https://www.cia.gov/library/publications/the-world-factbook/geos/ti.html (last visited Apr. 29, 2014), *archived at* http://perma.cc/H72P-LZLM.

[5] BURKHANOVA ET AL., *supra* note 1, at 37.

[6] LENA IONSON ET AL., RELIGIOZNII EKSTREMIZM V TSENTRAL'NOI AZII: PROBLEMI I PERSPEKTIVI [RELIGIOUS EXTREMISM IN CENTRAL ASIA: PROBLEMS AND PERSPECTIVES] 93 (Dushanbe, 2003) (in Russian).

II. Perception of Extremism

The Unified Concept of the Republic of Tajikistan on the Fight Against Terrorism and Extremism was introduced in 2006 by the decree of the Tajikistani President.[7] This Decree follows the scholarly approach toward extremism, which views extremism as a social phenomenon of the highest degree of intolerance that culminates in terrorism.[8] The phrase "terrorism and other forms of extremist manifestation" is used throughout the text of this Decree.

According to some Tajikistani scholars, extremism is based on the idea of group supremacy and feelings of contempt and hatred for those who are "below them" on the social ladder.[9] These scholars suggest that extremist ideas become dangerous when their adherents take concrete steps toward implementing them,[10] and that it is imperative to fight against such supremacist propaganda and the dissemination of extremist ideas, which inevitably engender hatred among various social groups.[11] Therefore, the core of the fight against extremism lies in prohibiting the "communication" of such ideas to others.[12] This fight is usually conducted through banning the activities of varied religious organizations that have been recognized as extremist. However, the government has not been transparent about how it reaches the determination of what constitutes "extremism" or "terrorism."[13]

The Law on the Fight Against Extremism (Antiextremism Law) was adopted by the Tajikistani legislature in 2003.[14] The Law defines extremism as "radical activity of individuals and organizations, aimed at destabilization, subverting the constitutional order in the country, seizing power, [or] inciting racial, national, social, or religious hatred."[15] The Law does not distinguish among various types of extremism, including religious extremism.

---

[7] Unified Concept of the Republic of Tajikistan on the Fight Against Terrorism and Extremism, Approved by the Decree of the President of Tajikistan No. 1717, (Mar. 28, 2006), *available at* http://www.geneva-academy.ch/RULAC/pdf_state/Concept-of-Combating-Terrorism-and-Extremism-TJ.pdf (in Russian), *archived at* http://perma.cc/9FZ2-CEQ2.

[8] DAVLIAT NAZIROV, RELIGIOZNO-POLITICHESKII EKSTREMIZM I TERRORIZM V TSENTRALNOI AZII [RELIGIOUS AND POLITICAL EXTREMISM AND TERRORISM IN CENTRAL ASIA] 6 (Dushanbe, 2003) (in Russian).

[9] *Id.* at 15.

[10] *Id.* at 6.

[11] *Id.*

[12] *Id.* at 15.

[13] *Central Asia: Overview of Key Human Rights Concerns and Recommendations: Tajikistan*, HUMAN RIGHTS WATCH (Nov. 15, 2012), http://www.hrw.org/news/2012/11/15/central-asia-overview-key-human-rights-concerns-and-recommendations (scroll down to "Tajikistan"), *archived at* http://perma.cc/Y9L8-MV2L.

[14] Law of the Republic of Tajikistan on the Fight Against Extremism [Antiextremism Law], adopted on Nov. 21, 2003 *available at* http://mmk.tj/ru/library/zakon_respubliki_tadzhikistan_o_borbe_s_ekstremizmom.doc (in Russian), *archived at* http://perma.cc/E7Q6-HDRW.

[15] *Id.* art. 3.1 (translated by the author).

III. Legal Framework for Fighting Extremism

A. Domestic Legislation

Provisions countering extremism can be found in various Tajikistani legal acts. Article 8 of the Constitution of Tajikistan states that "[t]he establishment and activity of public associations and political parties which encourage racism, nationalism, social and religious enmity, and hatred, as well as advocate the forcible overthrow of the constitutional state structures and the formation of armed groups shall be prohibited."[16] Similar norms are included in other laws. The Law on Freedom of Conscience and Religious Associations (Freedom of Religion Law) prohibits provoking religious-based hatred, enmity, or conflict, as well as humiliating and harming the religious sentiments of other citizens.[17]

While regulating freedom of religion, the state acknowledges its responsibility for conducting tolerance-building policies and preventing religious fanaticism and extremism.[18] This is why the state pays special attention to the way freedom of religion is implemented. The government believes that in order to fight extremism and prevent extremist manifestations and fanatic expressions, it is important to maintain control over the exercise of religious freedom, religious education, and circulation of religious literature.[19] This point of view is not supported by the civil society, however. International NGOs claim that Tajikistani authorities interfere with the exercise of freedom of religion, and sometimes exceed the limits of necessity in fighting extremism and terrorism. They report that the "government policy establishing far-reaching controls over religious education and worship goes hand in hand with the restrictions on general religious freedoms, including traditional Muslim and minority Christian beliefs."[20]

According to Human Rights Watch, in recent years the Tajikistani government has destroyed a synagogue, a church, and three mosques, and has closed down hundreds of unregistered mosques. In August 2012, media reported that Tajikistan's Committee on Religious Affairs, a government agency, had launched the installation of surveillance cameras in mosques, and that 40% of mosques had already been equipped with the cameras. Tajikistani authorities have also placed a ban on minority Muslim and Christian groups on the grounds that they are involved in "extremist" activities.[21] Besides the restrictions previously mentioned, the government interferes

---

[16] CONSTITUTION OF THE REPUBLIC OF TAJIKISTAN, adopted Nov. 6, 1994, amended June 22, 2003, English translation available on the President of Tajikistan website, *at* http://www.president.tj/en/taxonomy/term/5/28, *archived at* http://perma.cc/VD6G-AN5J.

[17] Law of the Republic of Tajikistan on Freedom of Conscience and Religious Associations [Freedom of Religion Law], adopted on Mar. 12, 2009, art. 4.5, *available at* http://mmk.tj/ru/library/o_svobode_sovesti_religioznih.doc (in Russian), *archived at* http://perma.cc/WZF5-9LRV.

[18] *Id.* art. 5.5.2.

[19] NARGIZ ZOKIROVA ET AL., THE HUMAN RIGHTS SITUATION IN TAJIKISTAN, 2011, at 32 (Human Rights and Rule of Law Bureau, 2011) (in Russian), *available at* http://ngoyonc_files.wordpress.com/2012/03/d0b5d0b6d0b5d0b3d0bed0b4d0bdd0b8d0ba_2011_d180d183d181d181-d0b2d0b5d180d181d0b8d18f.pdf, *archived at* http://perma.cc/W4QF-MR3N (click "Uploaded page" tab).

[20] *Id.* (translation by the author).

[21] HUMAN RIGHTS WATCH, *supra* note 13.

with citizens conducting religious rites and pilgrimages,[22] and restricts those who are suspected of association with extremist organizations from entering the country.[23]

Relevant provisions of the country's Criminal Code and Code of Administrative Violations are used for punishing extremist activities.

B. International Treaties and Cooperation

Tajikistan's participation in regional international organizations, such as the Shanghai Cooperation Organization, Collective Security Treaty Organization, and the Commonwealth of Independent States, defines the methods used by the country to fight against extremism. The Shanghai Convention on Combating Terrorism, Separatism and Extremism outlines the major principles guiding activities in this field. It describes extremism as "any activity aimed at the violent seizure of power or violent holding of power, and at the violent subversion of the constitutional order of the state, as well as the violent encroachment on public security, including the establishment of an organization or illegal armed groups for this purpose, or participation in [such activities]."[24] The Convention requires that such activities be criminally prosecuted according to the national legislation of the parties to the Convention.[25] This broad conception of extremism and reference to the national legislation of the member states implies that the goal of the Convention is not to create a uniform approach toward the fight against extremism, but rather to facilitate cooperation between the member states in prosecuting the crimes mentioned without limiting the states' independence.[26] The Convention emphasizes the member states' obligation to cooperate in the sphere of preventing, discovering, and countering activities considered extremist using means provided by national legislation.[27]

Bilateral international treaties related to fighting extremism have been signed with China, Kazakhstan, Kyrgyzstan, and Uzbekistan. These agreements address regional specifics of fighting terrorism, separatism, and extremism; regulating the exchange of information on individuals involved in religious extremism, transnational organized crime, and other threats to the stability and security of the parties; defining measures aimed at preventing such individuals from crossing state borders; and formulating rules for conducting joint actions, including military actions.[28]

---

[22] Freedom of Religion Law arts. 20–21.

[23] *Id.* art. 9.5.

[24] Shanghai Convention on Combating Terrorism, Separatism and Extremism art. 1.1.3, June 15, 2001, *available at* http://infoshos.ru/ru/?id=86 (in Russian) (translation by the author), *archived at* http://perma.cc/KM4E-XR3J.

[25] *Id.*

[26] Vladimir Antipenko, *Institutional Mechanism of Fighting Terrorism*, GOSUDARSTVO I PRAVO No. 11, at 70 (2004) (in Russian).

[27] Shanghai Convention, *supra* note 24, art. 2.2.

[28] Organization of Security and Cooperation in Europe, *Responses by the Delegation of Tajikistan to the Questionnaire on the Code of Conduct on Politico-Military Aspects of Security* (Apr. 20, 2012), *available at* http://www.osce.org/ru/fsc/90094?download=true (in Russian), *archived at* http://perma.cc/UX3G-AS3B.

IV. Methods Used to Fight Extremism

A. Control over Religious Education

Religious education is regulated within the framework of fighting extremism. In a 2011 speech, Tajikistan's President, Emomali Rakhmon, stated that it is the common responsibility of parents, scholars, and the clergy to build a peaceful society, and expressed concerns that those who study in religious schools abroad have more chances to become terrorists and extremists than mullahs or religious workers.[29]

This statement corresponds with the policy implemented by the Tajikistani government. On August 2, 2011, the President signed the Law on Responsibility of Parents for Educating and Raising Their Children.[30] The Law states that parents must not allow persons under eighteen (who are referred to as children) to watch pornography and films containing violent, extremist, and terrorist scenes; read and disseminate books, pamphlets, newspapers, journals, or electronic text messages containing pornography and violent, extremist, or terrorist content; and participate in religious associations, except when they are officially enrolled in a religious institution.[31] In addition, parents must not allow their children to study abroad unless they have received approval from authorized agencies.[32] Parents who fail to comply with the requirements of this Law are subject to severe legal penalties (including fines and imprisonment) under the Tajikistan Criminal Code's provision against obstructing compulsory education.[33]

Tajikistani police authorities have reportedly initiated criminal cases against individuals whose minor children are studying in Islamic religious schools in foreign Muslim countries.[34] According to Abdulakhin Kholikov, Chairman of the government's Religious Affairs Committee, almost 2,400 school-age children were studying at religious schools abroad at the beginning of 2011, and 1,870 of them returned home recently. Half of the students reported upon returning home that the teachers at these foreign religious schools had attempted to recruit them for violent Islamic groups.[35]

---

[29] *First Criminal Cases Against Parents Whose Children Are Studying Abroad Are Initiated in Tajikistan*, NEWSRU.COM (Apr. 13, 2011), at http://www.newsru.com/religy/13apr2011/tajikistan.html (in Russian), *archived at* http://perma.cc/U7KT-HEXE.

[30] Law of the Republic of Tajikistan on the Responsibility of Parents for Educating and Raising their Children, adopted on Aug. 2, 2011, *available at* http://mmk.tj/ru/library/ob_otvetstvennosti_roditelei_za_obuchenie_i_vospitanie_detei.doc (in Russian), *archived at* http://perma.cc/SMW3-MPM8.

[31] *Id.* art. 8.

[32] *Id.* art. 9.

[33] NEWSRU.COM, *supra* note 29; CRIMINAL CODE OF THE REPUBLIC OF TAJIKISTAN, adopted on May 21, 1998, art. 164, *available at* http://mmk.tj/ru/library/ugolovnii_kodeks_cht.doc (in Russian), *archived at* http://perma.cc/68E7-V27M, unofficial English translation *available at* http://legislationline.org/download/action/download/id/1707/file/207b8150765af2_c85ad6f5bb8a44.htm/preview, *archived at* http://perma.cc/84NC-VDNC.

[34] NEWSRU.COM, *supra* note 29.

[35] *Id.*

In 2013 at a meeting with youth, President Rakhmon addressed the involvement of young people in terrorist and extremist Islamist parties and movements, and the detention of dozens of these young "extremists" by Tajikistani police. According to the President, Tajikistani authorities are aware of the fact that some young people are involved in alien religious movements and groups, and are "taking steps to solve this problem."[36]

Religious education is addressed by the Law on Freedom of Conscience and Religious Associations. It states that children aged seven to eighteen are permitted to receive religious education within the country upon written consent of their parents or other representatives. Such education must not interfere with general public education. All religious educational establishments must be licensed.[37] In July 2013, five out of six existing Islamic religious schools (madrasas) in Tajikistan were temporarily closed for not having licenses to provide religious education.[38]

The Amendments of June 28, 2011, to the Freedom of Religion Law regulate religious education abroad.[39] The Amendments followed the President's request of August 25, 2010, that all Tajikistanis studying abroad return home.[40] In 2013 Tajikistani authorities announced that 1.6 thousand people who had been illegally enrolled in religious studies abroad were brought back to the country.[41] Reportedly, more than 620 people have been detained in Tajikistan over the past five years after being accused of joining various terrorist organizations and extremist movements following their graduation from unrecognized religious schools in foreign countries.[42]

Religious education abroad is not prohibited in Tajikistan, but it is subject to a number of specific requirements, such as prior religious education in Tajikistan and the written consent of the authorized government agency for regulating religious affairs.[43] Noncompliance with the provisions requiring authorization to teach religion is punishable by fines of up to the equivalent

---

[36] *Tajik President Emomali Rakhmon Concerned with Facts of Youth Involvement in Terrorist and Extremist Parties and Movements*, ASIA-PLUS (May 23, 2013), http://news.tj/ru/node/145850 (in Russian), *archived at* http://perma.cc/UJN9-X7YK.

[37] Freedom of Religion Law art. 8.

[38] *Studies for 300 Students from Sogdian Madrassas Suspended*, RADIO OZODI (July 12, 2013), http://rus.ozodi.org/content/five-tajik-medreseh-in-sughd-region-temporarily-closed/25044427.html (in Russian), *archived at* http://perma.cc/P2KQ-VEKA.

[39] Freedom of Religion Law art. 8.6.

[40] *Tajikistani Prosecutor General's Office Is Dissatisfied with the Work [Being Done] with Youth Returning from Religious Educational Institutions Abroad*, ISLAM IN SNG.COM (June 19, 2012), http://www.islamsng.com/tjk/news/4920 (in Russian), *archived at* http://perma.cc/CF6V-AJU2.

[41] *Id.*

[42] *More Than 620 Terrorists and Extremists Detained in Tajikistan over the Past Five Years*, COUNTER-TERROR.KZ (Jan. 24, 2013), http://counter-terror.kz/ru/article/view?id=163 (in Russian), *archived at* http://perma.cc/27QM-D7ZP (click "Screen capture" tab).

[43] Freedom of Religion Law art. 8.6.

of US$3,360.[44] Tajikistani citizens who violate the provision against receiving religious education abroad can be fined an amount equivalent to US$420–840.[45]

B. Control Over the Circulation of Religious Literature and Related Items

The government also controls the production and distribution of religious literature and related items with the aim of preventing extremism in Tajikistan. The Freedom of Religion Law provides for state theological evaluation and authorization of the production, export, import, sale, and distribution of religious literature and other related items.[46] Religious literature and related items must display the name of the religious organization producing it.[47]

The state theological evaluation is conducted by an authorized government agency in order to identify the specifics of the teachings of certain religious organizations, obtain correct information regarding their doctrine and practices, and review the content of their literature and items of religious significance.[48] The unauthorized publishing, export, import, sales, and distribution of religious literature is a misdemeanor under the Code of Administrative Violations[49] and is punishable by fines, which were substantially increased in 2011.[50] A special provision of the Code outlaws producing, stockpiling, importing, transporting, and distributing banned media products or other banned published materials. Violations of this provision are punishable by fines up to US$3,360, with confiscation of the items in question.[51] Even stricter fines are imposed for opening unregistered religious publishing houses.[52]

V. Punishment for Extremist Activities

A. Responsibility of Individuals

A variety of activities containing elements of extremism can qualify as crimes or administrative violations under Tajikistani legislation. Punishment for such activities differs depending on whether the perpetrator is an ordinary person or an official of a public organization, the

---

[44] CODE OF ADMINISTRATIVE VIOLATIONS OF THE REPUBLIC OF TAJIKISTAN, adopted Dec. 31, 2008, art. 474, *available at* http://mmk.tj/ru/library/kodeks_ob_administrativnih__pravonarusheniyah.doc (in Russian), *archived at* http://perma.cc/YQK2-A9G7, unofficial English translation *available at* http://cis-legislation.com/document.fwx?rgn=26352 (full text by subscription only).

[45] *Id.*

[46] Freedom of Religion Law art. 22.3.

[47] *Id.*

[48] *Id.* art. 17.

[49] CODE OF ADMINISTRATIVE VIOLATIONS art. 474.

[50] *Penalties for Unlawful Dissemination of Religious Literature Stiffened in Tajikistan*, TREND.AZ (Jan. 2, 2011), http://www.trend.az/regions/casia/tajikistan/1806319.html (in Russian), *archived at* http://perma.cc/H9EC-EZR7.

[51] CODE OF ADMINISTRATIVE VIOLATIONS art. 474.

[52] *Id.* art. 474[1].

punishment being much more severe when the activity is carried out by an individual holding an official position in an organization.[53]

Criminal liability for extremist activity is regulated by the Criminal Code of Tajikistan. The core provisions against religious extremism can be found in article 189, entitled "Inciting National, Racial, Regional, or Religious Hatred." The definition of religious extremism includes "any actions aimed at inciting hatred based on national, racial, regional, or religious criteria[;] humiliation of national dignity[;] and propaganda of supremacy based on religion, nationality, [or] racial or regional origin, if these actions have been committed publicly or through mass media." Such actions are punishable by imprisonment for up to five years.[54]

It appears that the following three criteria must be met for an action to qualify as extremist:

- The ultimate purpose of committing the act must be inciting enmity and hatred toward various religious groups and conflicts among them.

- The hatred must be directed against a group or groups formed on such criteria as religion, race, ethnicity, etc., and not against an individual.

- The act must be committed publicly or through the use of mass media.[55]

Article 189 of the Criminal Code states that a hate crime that is committed more than once, employs violence or the threat of violence, involves the abuse of official position, is committed by a group of persons, or is based on a prearranged agreement must be considered an aggravating circumstance.[56] In addition, the commission of any crime out of racial or religious enmity is an aggravating circumstance and leads to a more severe punishment.[57] The intention to cause national, religious, regional, or racial hatred is also considered an aggravating circumstance for prosecuting other crimes listed in the Code: assassination (article 104), intentionally inflicting harm on a person's health (articles 110–112), torture (article 117), and desecration of dead bodies and graves (article 243).

Creating an extremist organization and participating in this organization's activities are also crimes under Tajikistani legislation.[58] Article 307[2] of the Criminal Code defines an extremist organization as a group of persons organized for the purpose of perpetrating crimes prosecuted under articles 157 (interfering with activities of religious associations), 158 (interfering with activities of nongovernmental organizations or political parties), 160 (disrupting meetings, assemblies, and rallies), 185 (setting up illegal armed groups), 188 (creating public disorder), 189 (inciting hatred), 237 (hooliganism), 237.1 (vandalism), 242 (destroying monuments), and 243 (desecration of dead bodies and graves), if these crimes are committed out of national, racial,

---

[53] *Id.* art. 462.2.

[54] CRIMINAL CODE OF THE REPUBLIC OF TAJIKISTAN art. 189.

[55] *Id.*

[56] *Id.*

[57] *Id.* art. 62.

[58] *Id.* art. 307[2].

political, ideological, or religious hatred. It is also considered a crime to manage such a group or a part of it, or to plan to commit the aforementioned crimes.

Creating an extremist organization is punishable by deprivation of freedom (criminal legislation provides for different forms of restrictions on freedom, e.g., arrest, imprisonment, obligatory labor, exile) for a term of five to eight years, with a prohibition on occupying certain positions for a period of between two and five years after the sentence has been served.[59] Participation in such organizations is also punishable by up to five years of imprisonment followed by a three-year period of occupational restrictions. Those who voluntarily end their participation in an extremist group are relieved of criminal responsibility "if they have not committed another crime." The motivation of hatred in committing these crimes is the most important factor qualifying their perpetrators for prosecution.[60]

Article 307[3] of the Criminal Code provides for the punishment of those engaged in activities related to banned political, religious, or nongovernmental organizations. The Code distinguishes between simple participation in such organizations and organizing their activities. Activists of the banned organizations can be imprisoned for up to eight years, with further professional restrictions for a term of up to five years.[61] Individual members of such organizations can be fined or imprisoned for a term of up to five years.[62] Motivation appears to be immaterial for prosecuting individuals under article 307[3].

Religious education or study groups recognized as extremist are specifically addressed by the Tajikistani Criminal Code. Managing such groups or taking part in their activities is punishable by imprisonment for no less than five and no more than eight years, with confiscation of personal assets.[63] Seemingly, the intention to commit a hate crime is not considered a motivation required to bring charges against a person taking part in studies provided by an extremist educational group. The Law is not clear whether prosecuting a person for studying with such a group first requires proving that the person understood the extremist character of the organization.

B. Responsibility of Organizations

The responsibility of organizations involved in extremist activities is established by the Antiextremism Law and the Freedom of Religion Law. Both Laws provide for enforcement measures such as the following: notifying an organization that activities it is conducting are considered extremist and impermissible in the opinion of the supervising government authority (impermissibility does not amount to illegality, however); issuing a warning to such an organization; banning an organization's activities; and liquidating a religious organization.[64]

---

[59] *Id.*

[60] *Id.*

[61] *Id.* art. 307[3]

[62] CRIMINAL CODE OF THE REPUBLIC OF TAJIKISTAN article 307[2].

[63] *Id.* art. 307[4].

[64] According to the Freedom of Religion Law, liquidation cannot be applied to religious communities because they do not have the status of a legal entity.

If there is a reason to suspect that an organization is preparing to engage in illegal actions of an extremist nature, and there are no grounds for bringing criminal charges, the Prosecutor General of Tajikistan or other subordinate prosecutor sends a notification to the organization, pointing out the impermissibility of committing such actions and stating the facts that have caused suspicion that illegal actions might be conducted.[65] Warnings are issued by the Prosecutor General or other subordinate prosecutors, or by a state agency designated to fight against extremism, in cases when government authorities discover facts demonstrating the existence of extremist elements in an organization's activity.[66] The warning must also identify measures that need to be taken to correct the situation and the time frame during which the situation must be rectified. Under law, this term cannot exceed one month from the day of the warning.[67] If during the time period specified in the warning the violation is not rectified, or another violation is committed by the same organization within a twelve-month period, the Prosecutor General must file a claim to the court for the liquidation of the organization or banning of the religious community.[68]

Notifications and warnings issued by the Prosecutor General and other government officials can be appealed in a lower-level court in the area where the organization is registered.

The liquidation of an organization or ban on a religious community can be imposed by the court for failing to rectify the violation indicated by the Prosecutor General in his warning during the specified time; for committing another violation within a twelve-month period after the warning has been issued; for conducting extremist activity that results in the violation of human rights, causing damage to people, their health, the environment, public security, or the economic interests of the state and individuals; or creating the threat of such damage.[69] During the court hearings on liquidating an organization or banning a religious community, the government may request the court to order the organization or community under trial to halt its activities until the court makes its decision.[70]

The penalties applicable to mass media outlets for disseminating extremist materials are similar to those imposed on other organizations.[71]

---

[65] Antiextremism Law art. 10.

[66] *Id.* art. 11.

[67] *Id.*

[68] *Id.* art. 11.

[69] *Id.* art. 12.

[70] *Id.* art. 13.

[71] *Id.* art. 14.

LEGAL PROVISIONS ON FIGHTING EXTREMISM: CHINA, PAKISTAN, RUSSIA AND TAJIKISTAN: COMPARATIVE SURVEY

	CHINA	PAKISTAN	RUSSIA	TAJIKISTAN
Definition	"Extremism" is not clearly defined in domestic law. There is no comprehensive counterterrorism law or a law fighting extremism. In 2011, "terrorist activities" were defined by the national legislative body as: acts that seriously endanger the society such as acts that cause or intend to cause the death or injury of an individual, the heavy losses of properties, the damage of public facilities or the disruption of social order by such means as violence, destruction or intimidation for the purposes of creating social panic, endangering public security or coercing the State organs or international organizations and the acts of instigating, funding or otherwise assisting in the above activities.	"Terrorism" means the use or threat of action where… the use or threat is designed to coerce and intimidate or overawe the Government or the public or a section of the public or community or sect or create a sense of fear or insecurity in society; or The use or threat is made for the purpose of advancing a religious, sectarian or ethnic cause. (*Sec. 6, Anti-Terrorism Act, 1997*)	Activity of non-governmental, religious and other organizations, mass media or individuals, aimed at planning, organizing and implementing actions aimed at forcible change of the foundations of the constitutional system and violation of integrity of the Russian Federation; public justification of terrorism and other terrorist activity; incitement of social, racial, ethnic or religious hatred; propaganda of exclusiveness, superiority or inferiority of an individual based on his/her social, racial, ethnic, religious or linguistic identity, or his/her attitude to religion; violation of rights, liberties and legitimate interests of an individual because of his/her social, racial, ethnic, religious or linguistic identity or attitude to religion; (*Article 1, Law of Russian Federation on Countering Extremist Activity*)	Radical activity of legal and natural entities, which call for destabilization, change of constitutional order in the country, seize of power in the country, causing racial, national, social or religious hatred. (*Article 3, Law on Fighting Extremism of Republic of Tajikistan*)
Core Legal Provision	The socialist system is the basic system of the People's Republic of China. Disruption of the	No core constitutional provision on extremism but the Constitution of Pakistan	Propaganda, promotion of social, national, and religious racial, national, and religious supremacy as well as propaganda	Creation and activity of assemblies advocating racial, national, social and religious

	China	Pakistan	Russia	Tajikistan
	socialist system by any organization or individual is prohibited. (*Article 1, Constitution of China*) Discrimination against and oppression of any ethnic groups are prohibited; any act which undermines the unity of the ethnic groups or instigates division is prohibited. (*Article 4, Constitution of China*) No one may make use of religion to engage in activities that disrupt public order, impair the health of citizens or interfere with the educational system of the State. (*Article 36, Constitution of China*)	stipulates: "the State shall discourage parochial, racial, tribal, sectarian and provincial prejudices among the citizens (*Article 33, The Constitution of Pakistan*)	promotion of social, racial, national, and religious enmity or instigation of such enmity shall be forbidden. (*Article 29, Constitution of Russia*)	hatred or calling for violent overthrowing of constitutional order and organization of armed groups shall be forbidden. (*Article 8, Constitution of Tajikistan*)
Legal Acts Governing the Field	Counterterrorism: Criminal Law; State Security Law. Two regulations mentioning "religious extremism": Regulation on Religious Affairs; Regulation on Broadcasting and Television Administration.	Anti-Terrorism Act, 1997 Pakistan Penal Code	Law on Countering Extremist Activity Criminal Code Code of Administrative Violations	Law on Fighting Extremism Law on Freedom of Conscience and on Religious Associations Law on Responsibility of Parents for Educating and Upbringing their Children Criminal Code Code of Administrative Violations
Ways of Enforcement	The State establishes national counterterrorism task force (leading institution) The counterterrorism leading institution determines lists of terrorist organizations and	Anti-Terrorism Act imposes criminal liability for acts of terrorism and acts intended or likely to stir up sectarian hatred Establishment of Anti-	Criminal liability for propaganda and instigation of hatred among social groups (criminal's motivation is the determining factor)	Control over religious education of children Control over circulation of religious literature Criminal liability for

China, Pakistan, Russia, Tajikistan: Fighting Extremism

	China	Pakistan	Russia	Tajikistan
	terrorists, which will be published by the Ministry of Public Security	Terrorism Courts (ATCs) Power of Federal Government to proscribe organizations concerned with terrorism, place organizations under observation, and list activists, office-bearers or associates of organizations concerned or suspected to be concerned with terrorism or sectarianism	propaganda and instigation of hatred among social groups (criminal's motivation is the determining factor) Criminal liability for participation in extremist organizations Dissolution and banning organizations conducting extremist activity.	Dissolution and banning organizations conducting extremist activity Blacklisting media publishing extremist materials.
International Obligations	Shanghai Convention (The "Three Forces" approach appeared in a national development plan prior to the establishment of the SCO in the same year) Bilateral agreements on combating Terrorism, Separatism and Extremism signed with Kyrgyzstan, Kazakhstan, Tajikistan, Uzbekistan, Pakistan, Turkmenistan, and Russia	Currently has observer status at SCO Seeking full membership Currently has bilateral Cooperation Agreement on Combating Terrorism, Separatism and Extremism with the People's Republic of China, signed on April 5, 2005	Shanghai Convention on Combating Terrorism, Separatism and Extremism Cooperation Agreement between Russia and China on Combating Terrorism, Separatism and Extremism	Shanghai Convention on Combating Terrorism, Separatism and Extremism Agreement with China on Cooperation in Fight Against Terrorism, Separatism and Extremism (Sept. 2, 2003) Treaty with Kazakhstan, Kyrgyzstan, and Uzbekistan on Joint Actions in Fighting Terrorism, Political and Religious Extremism, Transnational Organized Crime, and Other Threats to Stability and Security of the Parties (Apr. 21, 2000) SCO Agreement on Cooperation in Preventing Entry to Member States for persons participating in terrorism, separatism and extremism (June 15, 2006)